# Social Studies

## Daily Practice Workbook

### 20 weeks of fun activities

3rd

ARGOPREP

**History**

**Civics and Government**

**Geography**

**Economics**

I0519092

ArgoPrep is one of the leading providers of supplemental educational products and services. We offer affordable and effective test prep solutions to educators, parents and students. Learning should be fun and easy! To access more resources visit us at www.argoprep.com.

Our goal is to make your life easier, so let us know how we can help you by e-mailing us at: info@argoprep.com.

- ArgoPrep is a recipient of the prestigious **Mom's Choice Award**.

- ArgoPrep also received the 2019 **Seal of Approval** from Homeschool.com for our award-winning workbooks.

- ArgoPrep was awarded the 2019 **National Parenting Products Award, Gold Medal Parent's Choice Award** and **the Tillywig Brain Child Award**.

# SOCIAL STUDIES

Social Studies Daily Practice Workbook by ArgoPrep allows students to build foundational skills and review concepts. Our workbooks explore social studies topics in depth with ArgoPrep's 5 E's to build social studies mastery.

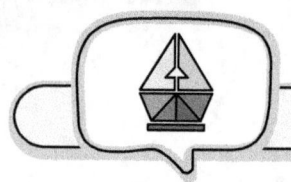
# Introduction

Welcome to our third grade social studies workbook!

This workbook has been specifically designed to help students build mastery of foundational social studies skills that are taught in third grade. Included are 20 weeks of comprehensive instruction covering the four branches of social studies: Geography, History, Civics and Government, and Economics.

This workbook dedicates five weeks of instruction to each of the four branches of social studies, focusing on different standards within each week of instruction.

Within the branch of Geography, students will learn about the world community and understand topics such as maps and models. They will also learn about timelines. The second branch is History, where students will make connections between their own environment and the past. In Civics and Government, they will learn more about community helpers and what it means to be a citizen.Finally, in the Economics section, they will have the opportunity to learn about different jobs and basic economic needs.

At the conclusion of the 20 weeks of instruction, students should have a solid grasp of the concepts required by the National Council for Social Studies for third grade.

## Table of Contents

## How to Use the Book

All 20 weeks of daily activity pages in this book follow the same weekly structure. The book is divided into four sections: Geography, History, Civics and Government, and Economics. The activities in each of the sections align to the recommendations of the National Council for the Social Studies which will help prepare students for state standardized assessments. While the sections can be completed in any order, it is important to complete each week within the section in chronological order since the skills often build upon one another.

Each week focuses on one specific topic within the section. More information about the weekly structure can be found in the Weekly Planner section.

## Weekly Planner

| Day | Activity | Description |
|---|---|---|
| 1 | Engaging with the Topic | Read a short text on the topic and answer multiple choice questions. |
| 2 | Exploring the Topic | Interact with the topic on a deeper level by collecting, analyzing and interpreting information. |
| 3 | Explaining the Topic | Make sense of the topic by explaining and beginning to draw conclusions about information. |
| 4 | Experiencing the Topic | Investigate the topic by making real-life connections. |
| 5 | Elaborating on the Topic | Reflect on the topic and use all information learned to draw conclusions and evaluate results. |

## How to access video explanations?

 Go to **argoprep.com/social3** OR scan the QR Code:

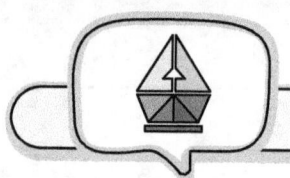
# List of Topics

| Unit | Week | Topic |
|---|---|---|
| Geography | 1 | World Communities |
| Geography | 2 | Landforms |
| Geography | 3 | Bodies of Water |
| Geography | 4 | Maps & Globes |
| Geography | 5 | World Explorers |
| History | 6 | World Settlers |
| History | 7 | Cultures & Traditions: Past and Present |
| History | 8 | Arts, Music & Dance |
| History | 9 | Folktales |
| History | 10 | World Languages |
| Civics & Government | 11 | World Leaders |
| Civics & Government | 12 | Laws |
| Civics & Government | 13 | Citizenship |
| Civics & Government | 14 | Rights & Responsibilities |
| Civics & Government | 15 | Human Rights |
| Economics | 16 | Basic Needs & Wants |
| Economics | 17 | Natural Resources |
| Economics | 18 | Goods & Services |
| Economics | 19 | Producers & Consumers |
| Economics | 20 | World Resources |

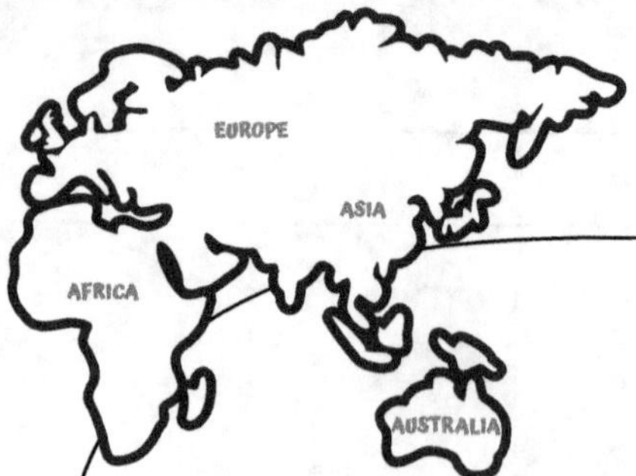

# WEEK 1

# Geography
## World Communities

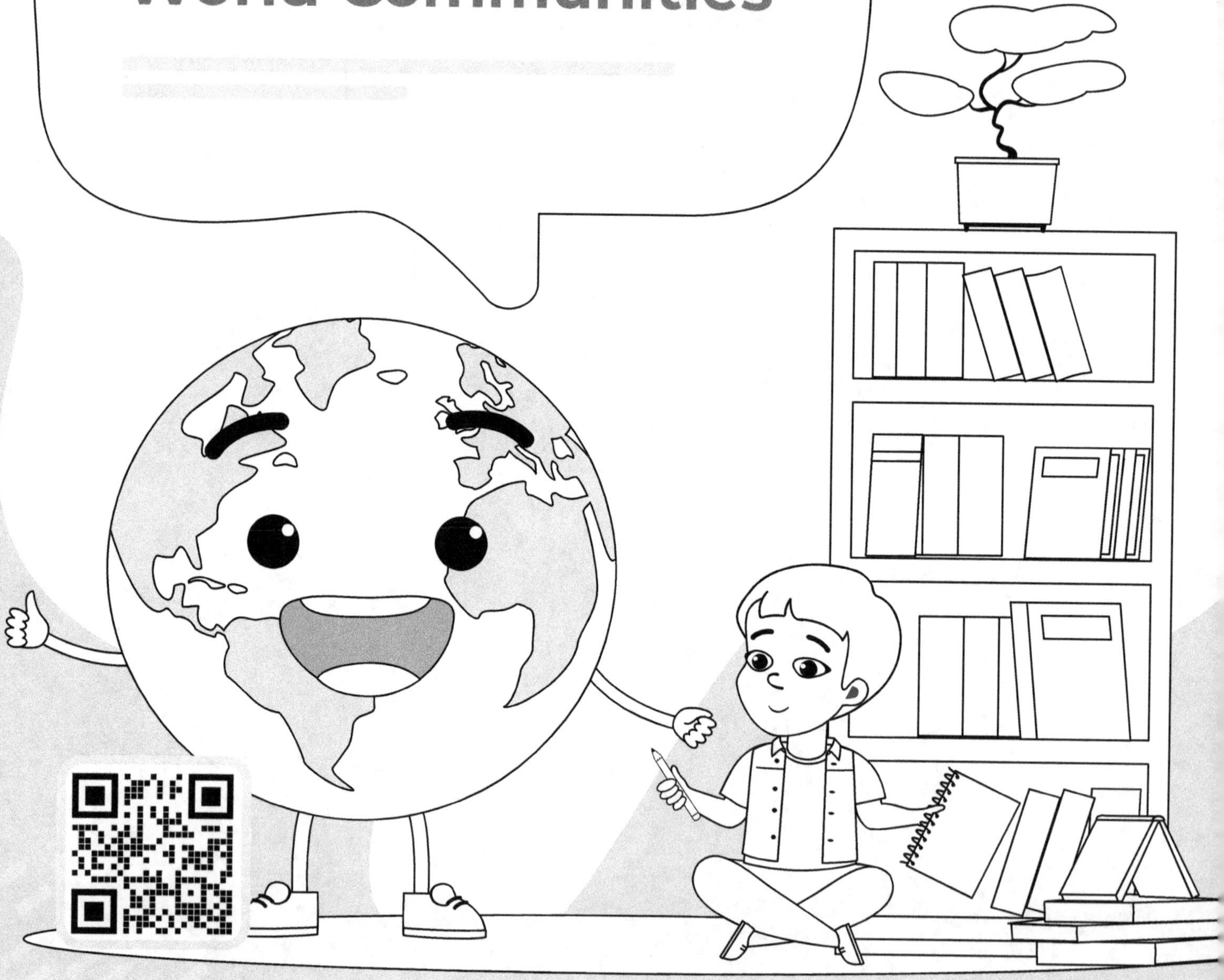

Learn about large and small communities on Earth.

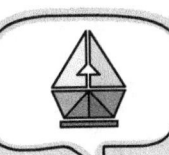
**Directions:** Read the text below. Then answer the questions that follow.

> The **world** is a very big place. It is made up of all the people, places and nature on Earth. A **community** is a group of people living in the same place. There are small communities such as schools, neighborhoods, and cities. A **global** community includes the whole world. Everyone who lives on the planet Earth is part of this community. There are over 7 billion people in the world!

1. The world is all the people, places and nature ......................................... .

    **A.** in your neighborhood
    **B.** in a large country
    **C.** on the planet Earth
    **D.** on a small continent

2. What is a global community?

    **A.** everyone in the world
    **B.** everyone in the same country
    **C.** everyone who attends the same school
    **D.** everyone who lives in a small community

3. How many people live on the planet Earth?

    **A.** 10,000
    **B.** 65,000
    **C.** 2,000,000
    **D.** 7,000,000,000

4. How can people who live in different countries be part of the same community?

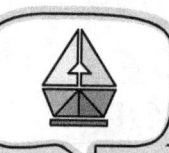
*Yesterday you learned about global communities. Everyone on Earth is part of this community. Today you will learn about smaller parts of the world community.*

**Directions:** Read the text below. Then answer the questions that follow.

**Continents** are very large areas of land. There are 7 continents on Earth. They are: Asia, Africa, North America, South America, Antarctica, Europe, and Australia. These continents are all part of the global community. Each continent is its own community as well.

Continents vary in size and **population**. Population is the number of people living in a specific area. For example, Australia is the smallest continent in the world. Its population is about 25 million. Asia is the largest continent. Over 4 billion people live in Asia.

1. Which of these is one of the 7 continents?

   **A.** The United States of America

   **B.** Italy

   **C.** Europe

   **D.** Atlantic Ocean

2. Population is the _____ of people living in a specific area.

   **A.** community

   **B.** number

   **C.** area

   **D.** type

3. What is the population of Australia?

   **A.** about 25,000,000

   **B.** less than 25,000

   **C.** over 25,000,000,000

   **D.** under 2,500

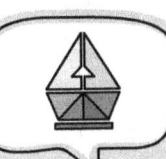
**Directiцons:** Read the text below. Then answer the questions that follow.

Remember that a global community is very large. There are smaller communities within the world community. Yesterday you learned about continents. You know that each continent is its own community. Now you will take a deeper look into those communities.

There are 300 million people on the continent of North America. They all live on the same continent but in different countries. There are 23 countries in North America. The United States of America has the biggest population. There are 50 states in the USA. Each state has its own city communities.

Look at the diagram below. It shows communities within a global community.

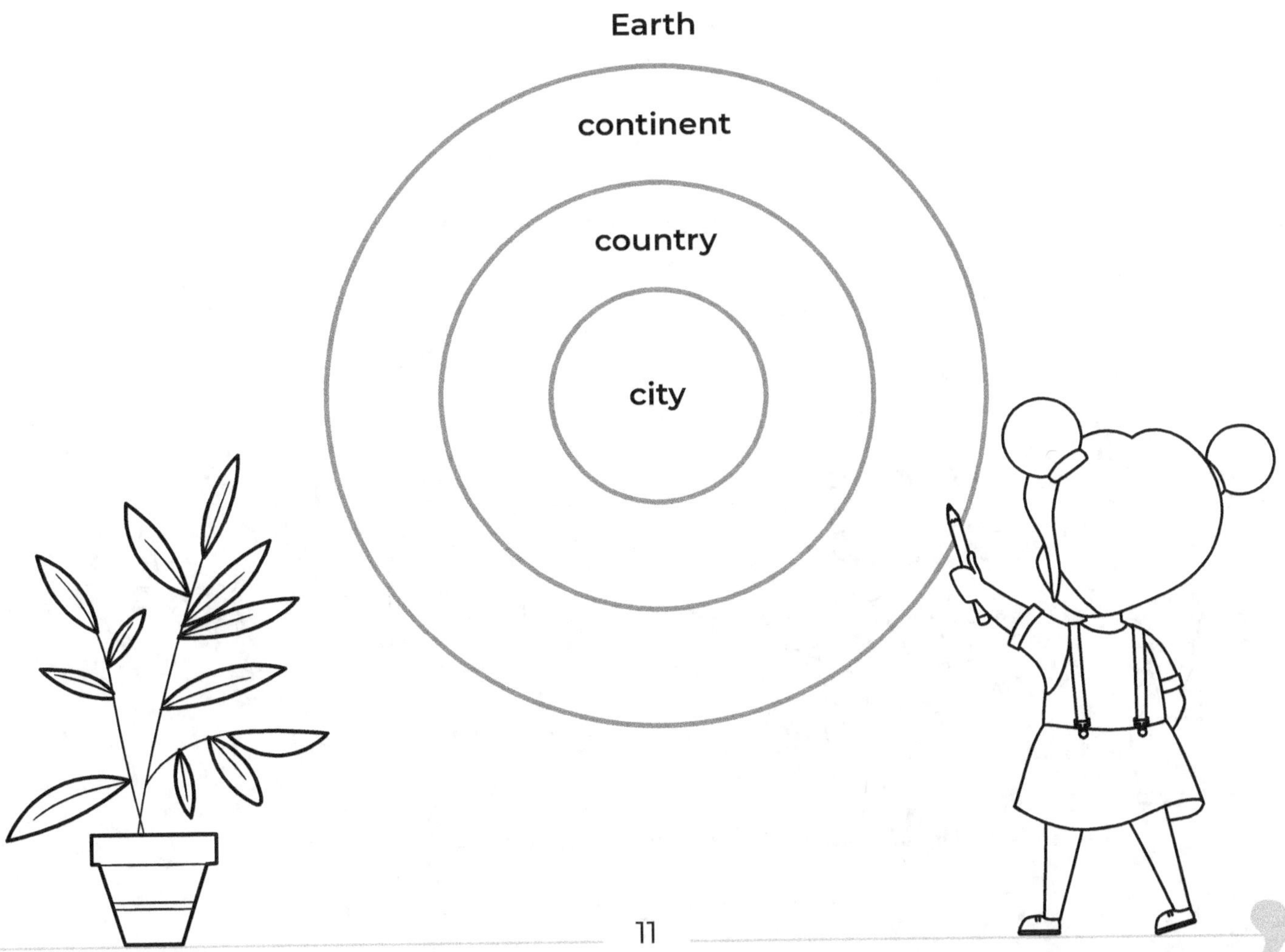

**Earth**

**continent**

**country**

**city**

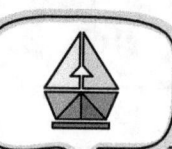
Pick a continent that you want to know more about. Learn more about the communities on that continent. Fill in the information below and complete the diagram.

continent: ...........................................

country: ...........................................

city: ...........................................

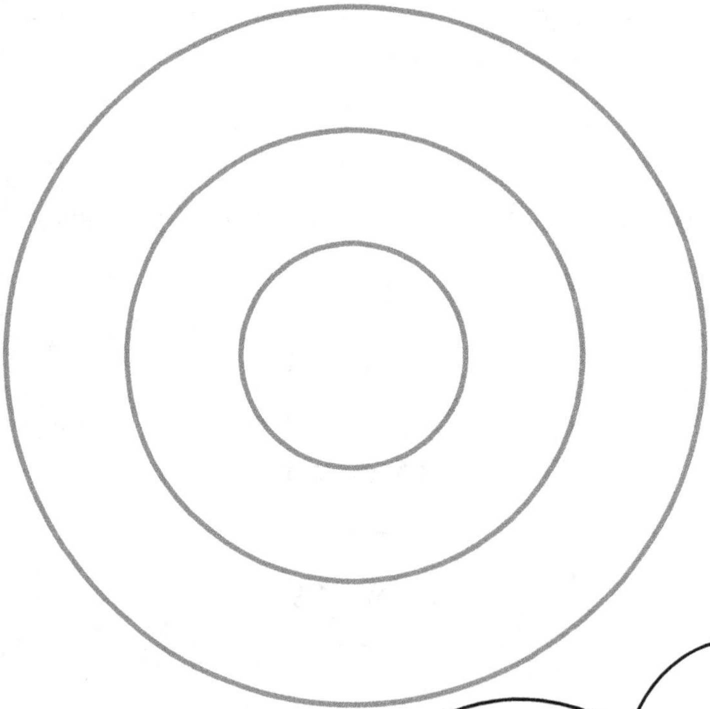

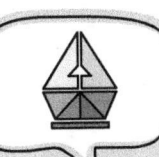
**Directions**: Read the text below. Then answer the questions that follow.

> You know continents are part of the global community. Each continent has its own communities. These continents also have special characteristics and features. For example, Antarctica is extremely cold and windy. The population there is less than 5,000 people. Antarctica is known for its huge icy mountains and freezing lakes.

What continent do you live on? Use resources such as the Internet, almanac, etc. to find the following information:

I live on the continent ................................................................ .

What is the population? ................................................................

Name 3 countries on this continent.

................................................................................................

................................................................................................

................................................................................................

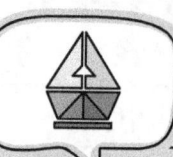
Which communities within this continent do you live in?

.................................................................................................................................

.................................................................................................................................

.................................................................................................................................

Find a fun fact about this continent. Write it below.

.................................................................................................................................

.................................................................................................................................

.................................................................................................................................

.................................................................................................................................

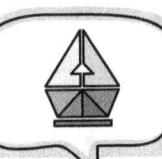
**Directions:** Read the text below. Then answer the questions that follow.

This week you learned about world communities. Today you will answer a few more questions about what you've learned.

1.  Which of these communities is the smallest?

    **A.** a global community
    **B.** a community in New York City
    **C.** the continent of South America
    **D.** The United States of America

2.  Which of these is NOT a continent?

    **A.** Alabama
    **B.** Asia
    **C.** Antarctica
    **D.** Africa

3.  True or false?

    North America is a small continent. It has a population of only 300 people.

    **A.** true
    **B.** false

4.  Explain how there can be smaller communities within a continent.

    ..............................................................................................................

    ..............................................................................................................

    ..............................................................................................................

    ..............................................................................................................

# WEEK 2

# Geography
## Landforms

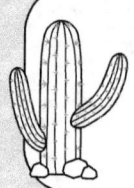

Explore various types of natural features on Earth.

ARGOPREP

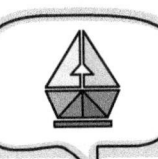
*Last week you learned about global communities. You know continents are part of the world community. Continents are very large areas of land. There are many types of land on Earth. This week you will learn about these* **landforms.**

**Directions:** Read the text below. Then answer the questions that follow.

A **landform** is a natural feature on the Earth's surface formed by acts of nature. A mountain is a type of landform. Mountains form when the Earth's **crust** is pushed upwards. This happens when **tectonic plates** move or get smashed together. A tectonic plate is a giant slab of rock under the Earth's surface.

Other landforms, such as hills and valleys, are caused by weather. Wind can blow small rocks and soil into a pile. Water can move quickly to form grooves on the Earth's surface.

**1.** A landform is a(n) ........................................ feature on the Earth's surface.

   **A.** man-made

   **B.** natural

   **C.** underground

   **D.** invisible

**2.** Which of these is a landform?

   **A.** hill

   **B.** ocean

   **C.** statue

   **D.** rainstorm

**3.** What are tectonic plates?

   **A.** mountains that are formed by wind

   **B.** piles of small rocks and soil

   **C.** slabs of rocks under the Earth's surface

   **D.** grooves that are formed by water

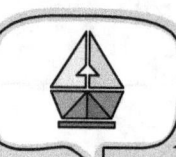
*Yesterday you learned about landforms. You know they are formed by nature. Today you will learn about more landforms and how they are formed.*

**Directions:** Read the text below. Then answer the questions that follow.

| landform | how it is formed |
|---|---|
| **mountain** | tectonic plates cause the Earth's crust to move upward |
| **hill** | rocks, soil or sand get pushed into a pile by nature (wind, water, etc.) |
| **valley** | rushing water (such as a river) moves and forms a groove in the Earth's surface |
| **canyon** | water moves for many years and forms a deep valley in the Earth's surface |
| **glacier** | large sheets of ice move slowly over land |

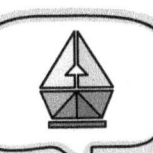
**1.** Which of these is formed by ice?

    **A.** glacier

    **B.** hill

    **C.** canyon

    **D.** valley

**2.** A ................................................ is a deep valley in the Earth's surface.

    **A.** mountain

    **B.** glacier

    **C.** hill

    **D.** canyon

**3.** How can water create landforms on Earth? List 2 landforms that can be formed by water.

.................................................................................................................................

.................................................................................................................................

.................................................................................................................................

.................................................................................................................................

**Directions:** Read the text below. Then answer the questions that follow.

> Remember that landforms can be caused by weather. **Erosion** is the process in which materials (such as soil and rocks) are moved from one place to another by water or wind. **Weathering** is when materials are broken down by weather.

Look at each picture below. Explain what is happening.

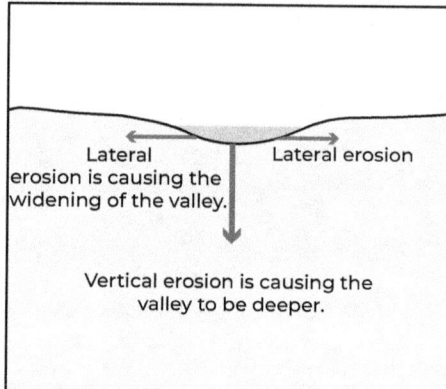

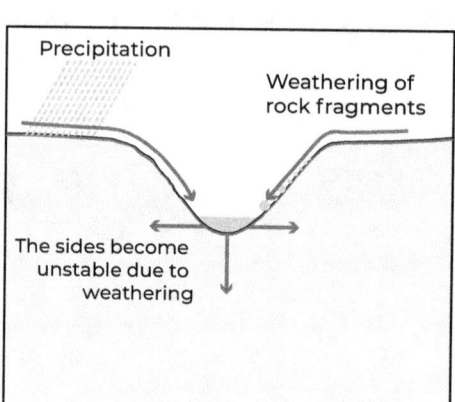

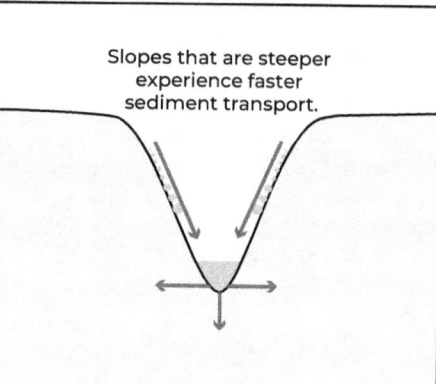

**1.** ...........................................................................................................................................

...........................................................................................................................................

...........................................................................................................................................

...........................................................................................................................................

...........................................................................................................................................

...........................................................................................................................................

Weathering causes the rock to break down

Erosion (from water or wind) moves the sediment downhill to another place

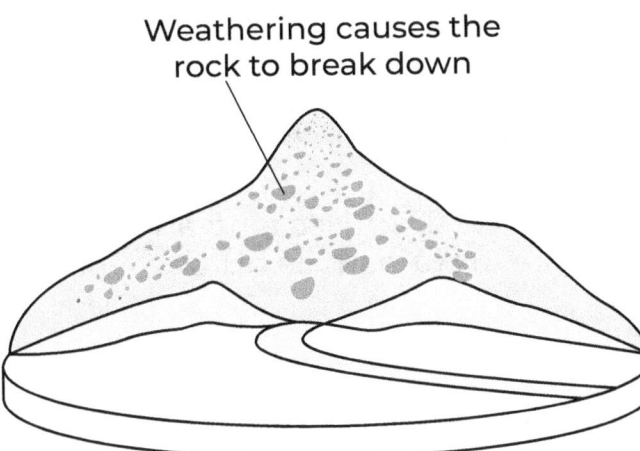

2. ..................................................................................................................................

.............................................................................................................................................

.............................................................................................................................................

.............................................................................................................................................

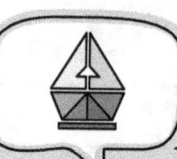
*On Day 2 you learned about canyons. You know they are formed when water moves through an area for many years. The pressure from the water forms a deep valley in the Earth's surface.*

**Directions:** Read the text below. Then answer the questions that follow.

The Grand Canyon is a famous canyon in Arizona. It is 277 miles long and 6,093 feet deep! How did the Grand Canyon form? Use resources to learn its history. Write what you learned below.

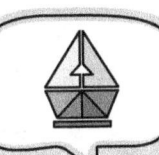
**Directions:** Read the text below. Then answer the questions that follow.

This week you learned about landforms and how they are formed. Today you will answer a few more questions about what you've learned.

1. Which of these is NOT a landform?

   **A.** valley

   **B.** road

   **C.** mountain

   **D.** canyon

2. What is weathering?

   **A.** when materials are broken down by weather

   **B.** when materials are moved from one place to another

   **C.** when materials move underneath the Earth's surface

   **D.** all of these

3. How deep is the Grand Canyon?

   **A.** 23 feet

   **B.** 500 feet

   **C.** 147 feet

   **D.** 6,093 feet

4. Explain how erosion can be caused by wind or water.

   ......................................................................................................................

   ......................................................................................................................

   ......................................................................................................................

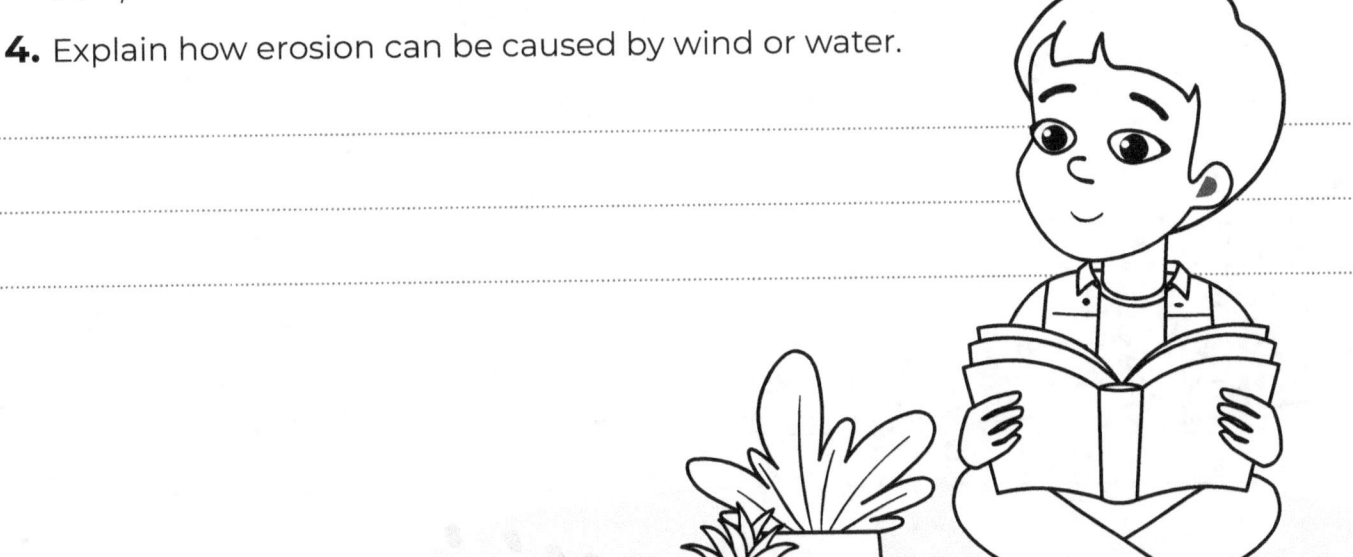

# WEEK 3

# Geography
## Bodies of Water

Identify various bodies of water on Earth.

ARGOPREP

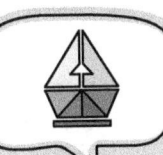
*Last week you learned about landforms. Remember that the Earth is made of land and water. This week you will learn about the **bodies of water** found on Earth.*

**Directions:** Read the text below. Then answer the questions that follow.

Did you know that 71% of Earth's surface is covered by water? Most of this water is found in **oceans**. Oceans are the largest bodies of water in the world. There are 4 main oceans: Atlantic, Pacific, Arctic and Indian. These oceans surround the 7 continents.

1. True or false?

   Most of the Earth's surface is covered by land.

   **A.** true
   **B.** false

2. Water covers ................................................ of the Earth's surface.

   **A.** 12
   **B.** 85
   **C.** 71
   **D.** 100

3. Which of these is 1 of the 4 main oceans?

   **A.** Colorado
   **B.** Pacific
   **C.** Nile
   **D.** Australia

4. Find out which oceans surround the continent of North America.

....................................................................................

....................................................................................

....................................................................................

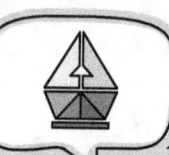
*Yesterday you learned about oceans. Oceans are the largest bodies of water on Earth. There are many other types of water bodies. Today you will learn about them.*

**Directions:** Read the text below. Then answer the questions that follow.

Look at the chart below.

| body of water | description |
|---|---|
| **stream** | a small, narrow river |
| **lake** | a large body of water surrounded by land |
| **pond** | a small body of still water |
| **river** | a large stream of water that flows into a larger body of water |
| **ocean** | a large body of saltwater |

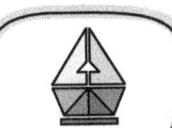
Now, look at each picture. Label the bodies of water based on their description.

**1.** ....................................................

**2.** ....................................................

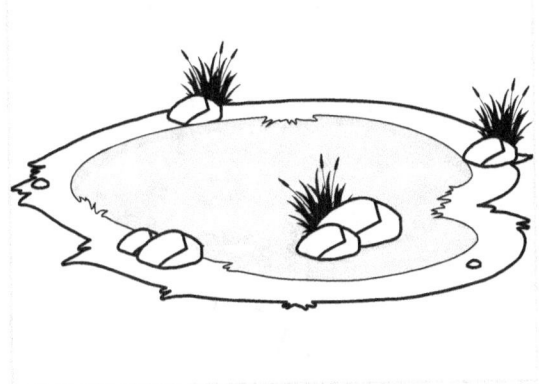

**3.** ....................................................

**4.** ....................................................

**5.** ....................................................

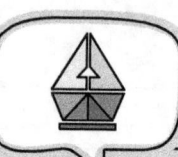
*Yesterday you learned about different types of water bodies. You know a river is a large stream of flowing water. Today you will learn about some famous rivers around the world.*

**Directions:** Read the text below. Then answer the questions that follow.

> The **Nile River** is the longest river in the world. It is over 4,000 miles long. The Nile River is located in Africa. It flows into the Mediterranean Sea. A **sea** is a large body of water but is smaller than an ocean. Seas are usually found near land.
>
> There are many rivers in North America. The **Mississippi River** is one of the major rivers on this continent. It runs through 10 states in America all the way to the Gulf of Mexico. A **gulf** is part of an ocean or sea that is surrounded by land.

**1.** Where is the Nile River located?

   **A.** North America

   **B.** Asia

   **C.** Africa

   **D.** South America

**2.** How many U.S. states does the Mississippi River run through?

   **A.** 12

   **B.** 10

   **C.** 29

   **D.** 41

**3.** Which of these is the largest?

   **A.** stream

   **B.** pond

   **C.** sea

   **D.** ocean

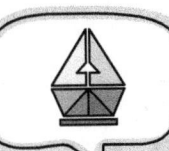
**Directions:** Read the text below. Then answer the questions that follow.

Do you live near a beach? Have you ever gone fishing in a nearby lake? Today you will think about bodies of water in your community.

**1.** Where do you live? What is the nearest river in your community?

.......................................................................................................................................

.......................................................................................................................................

.......................................................................................................................................

.......................................................................................................................................

**2.** Have you ever seen a pond? Where was it?

.......................................................................................................................................

.......................................................................................................................................

.......................................................................................................................................

.......................................................................................................................................

.......................................................................................................................................

.......................................................................................................................................

.......................................................................................................................................

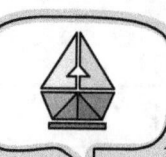
**3.** Do you go swimming in your community? Where do you swim?

.....................................................................................................................

.....................................................................................................................

.....................................................................................................................

.....................................................................................................................

.....................................................................................................................

.....................................................................................................................

.....................................................................................................................

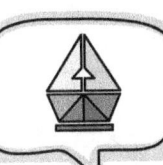
**Directions:** Read the text below. Then answer the questions that follow.

This week you learned about many different bodies of water. Today you will review them.

**1.** Most of Earth's water is found in ......................................... .

  **A.** oceans
  **B.** lakes
  **C.** streams
  **D.** rivers

**2.** A ......................................... is a small, narrow river.

  **A.** sea
  **B.** stream
  **C.** gulf
  **D.** lake

**3.** A ......................................... is a large body of water surrounded by land.

  **A.** ocean
  **B.** pond
  **C.** lake
  **D.** sea

**4.** The Mississippi River runs to the ......................................... of Mexico.

  **A.** Gulf
  **B.** Sea
  **C.** Ocean
  **D.** Stream

# WEEK 4

# Geography
## Maps & Globes

Discover the world with geography tools such as maps and globes.

ARGOPREP

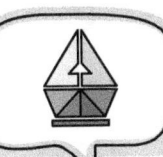
*You have learned about world communities over the past few weeks. You know that Earth is made up of land and water. You also know about various landforms and bodies of water. This week you will learn how to locate them.*

**Directions:** Read the text below. Then answer the questions that follow.

> Maps and globes are important **geography** tools. Geography is the study of Earth and its features. **Globes** give you a sphere-shaped view of the Earth. A **world map** is a flat picture of the Earth. Both globes and world maps can help you find continents and bodies of water.

1. What is geography?

   A. a special type of map used to study the Earth

   B. a person who studies the Earth

   C. the study of Earth and its features

   D. the study of maps and globes

2. Globes give you a ............................................ view of the Earth.

   A. flat

   B. one-dimensional

   C. small

   D. sphere-shaped

3. True or false?

   Maps should not be used to locate continents and oceans.

   A. true

   B. false

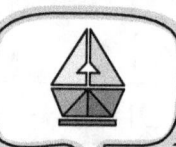
*Yesterday you learned about maps and globes. You can use these tools to find land and water on Earth. Today you will practice using a world map.*

**Directions:** Read the text below. Then answer the questions that follow.

"

Maps can help people travel around the world. The **compass rose** tells you which direction to travel in by showing you the **cardinal directions**: north, east, south and west.

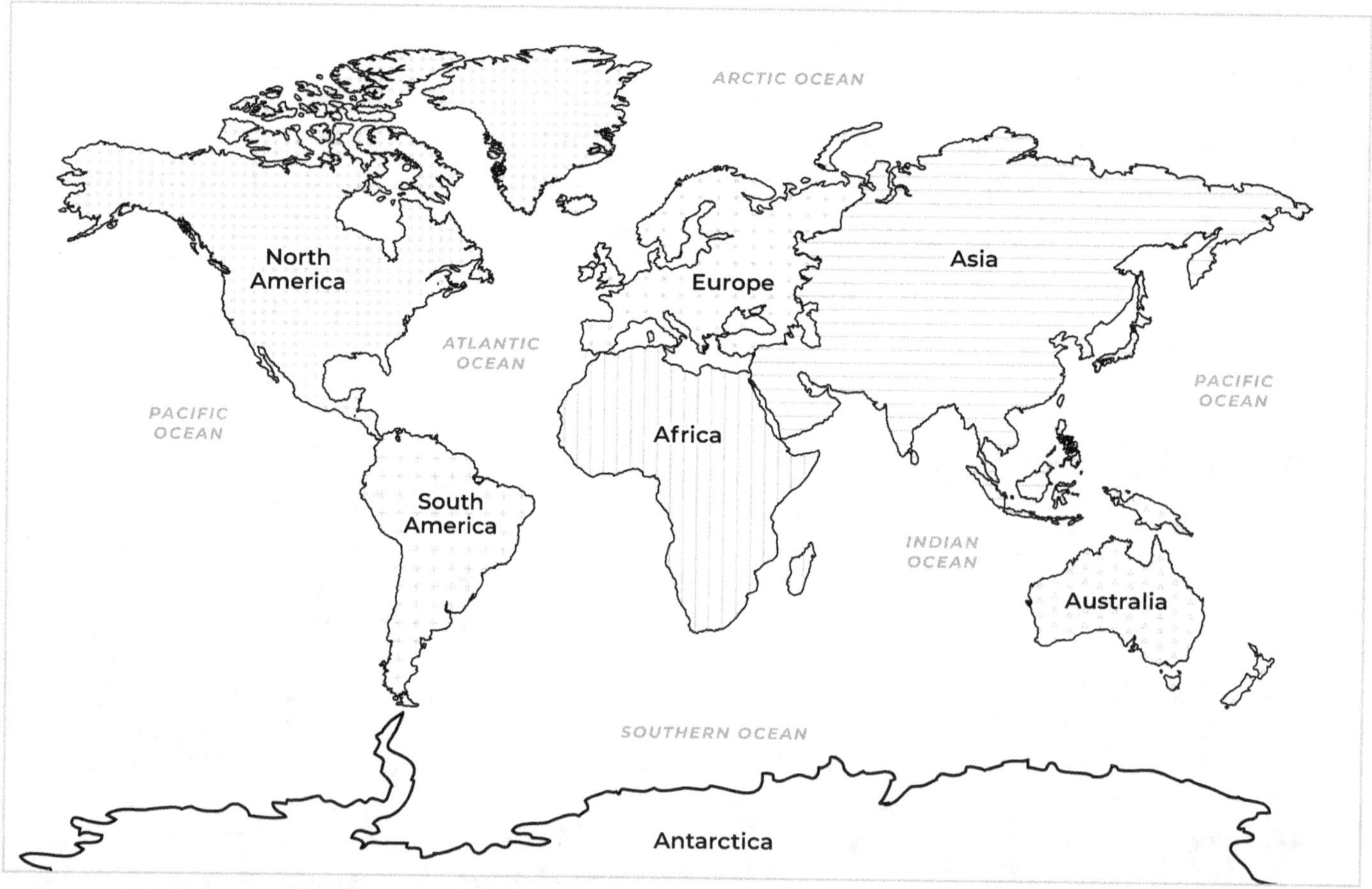

"

ARCTIC OCEAN

North America

Europe

Asia

ATLANTIC OCEAN

PACIFIC OCEAN

PACIFIC OCEAN

Africa

South America

INDIAN OCEAN

Australia

SOUTHERN OCEAN

Antarctica

**1.** Which continent is closest to Asia?

   **A.** Europe
   **B.** North America
   **C.** South America
   **D.** Antarctica

**2.** Where is the Indian Ocean?

   **A.** in between Africa and Australia
   **B.** above North America
   **C.** in between Africa and South America
   **D.** below Antarctica

**3.** Which continent is located south of Europe?

   **A.** Asia
   **B.** Africa
   **C.** North America
   **D.** all of these

**4.** In which direction would you travel to get from North America to Antarctica?

   **A.** north
   **B.** south
   **C.** east
   **D.** west

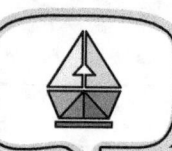
*Yesterday you located continents and oceans on a map. Maps can help you find other types of land and water on Earth. A **physical map** shows natural features such as mountains, rivers and lakes. The **map key** helps you find these features by showing you what each symbol represents.*

**Directions:** Read the text below. Then answer the questions that follow.

Look at the physical map below. It shows natural features in the United States.

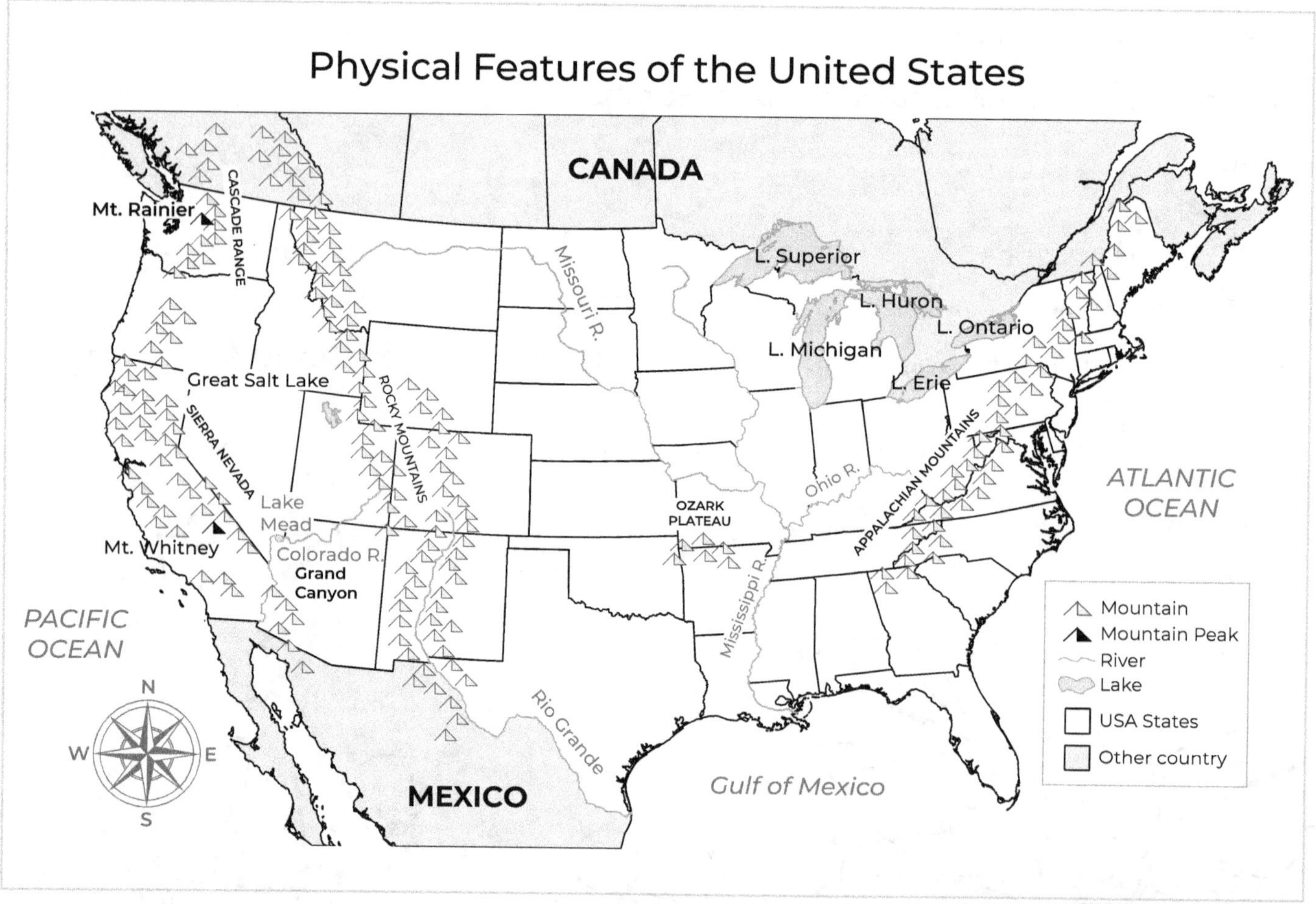

### Physical Features of the United States

CANADA

Mt. Rainier

CASCADE RANGE

Missouri R.

L. Superior

L. Huron

L. Michigan

L. Ontario

L. Erie

Great Salt Lake

ROCKY MOUNTAINS

SIERRA NEVADA

Lake Mead

Mt. Whitney

Colorado R.

Grand Canyon

OZARK PLATEAU

Ohio R.

APPALACHIAN MOUNTAINS

Mississippi R.

ATLANTIC OCEAN

PACIFIC OCEAN

Rio Grande

N
W      E
S

MEXICO

Gulf of Mexico

Map Key:
- Mountain
- Mountain Peak
- River
- Lake
- USA States
- Other country

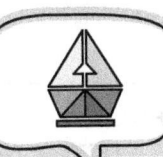
**1.** What type of landforms can you find on this map?

..................................................................................................................................

..................................................................................................................................

..................................................................................................................................

**2.** Name 2 bodies of water found on this map.

..................................................................................................................................

..................................................................................................................................

..................................................................................................................................

**3.** Explain how map keys can help you use a map.

..................................................................................................................................

..................................................................................................................................

..................................................................................................................................

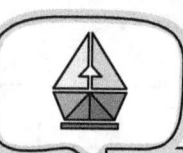
*You know a globe is sphere-shaped. It is shaped like the Earth. Today you will compare globes with real images of the planet Earth.*

**Directions:** Read the text below. Then answer the questions that follow.

Visit google.earth.com to see 3-D satellite pictures of Earth. Think about how it is like a globe. How are globes different from the real planet Earth? Use the Venn diagram below to compare and contrast.

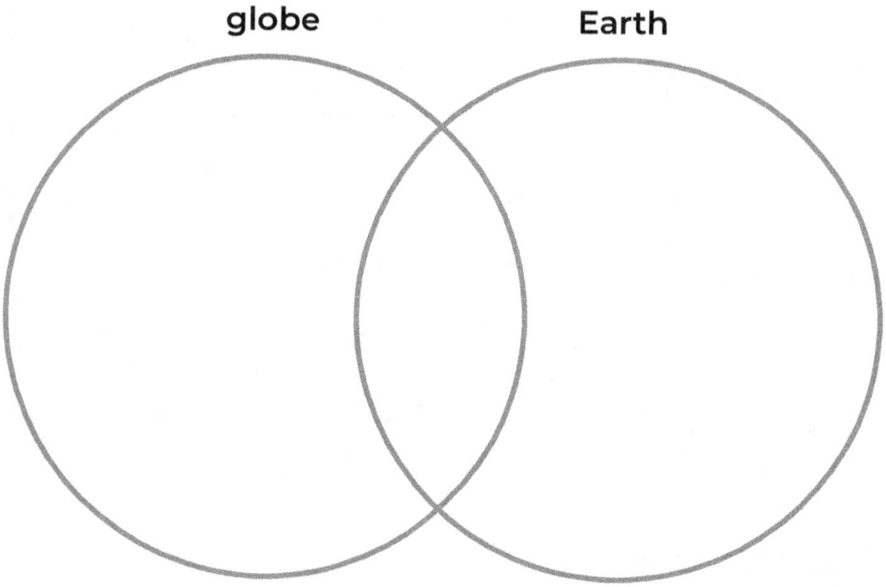

globe                    Earth

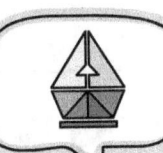
**Directions:** Read the text below. Then answer the questions that follow.

This week you learned about maps and globes. Today you will draw your own physical map of any area. Your map should have a compass rose and a key.

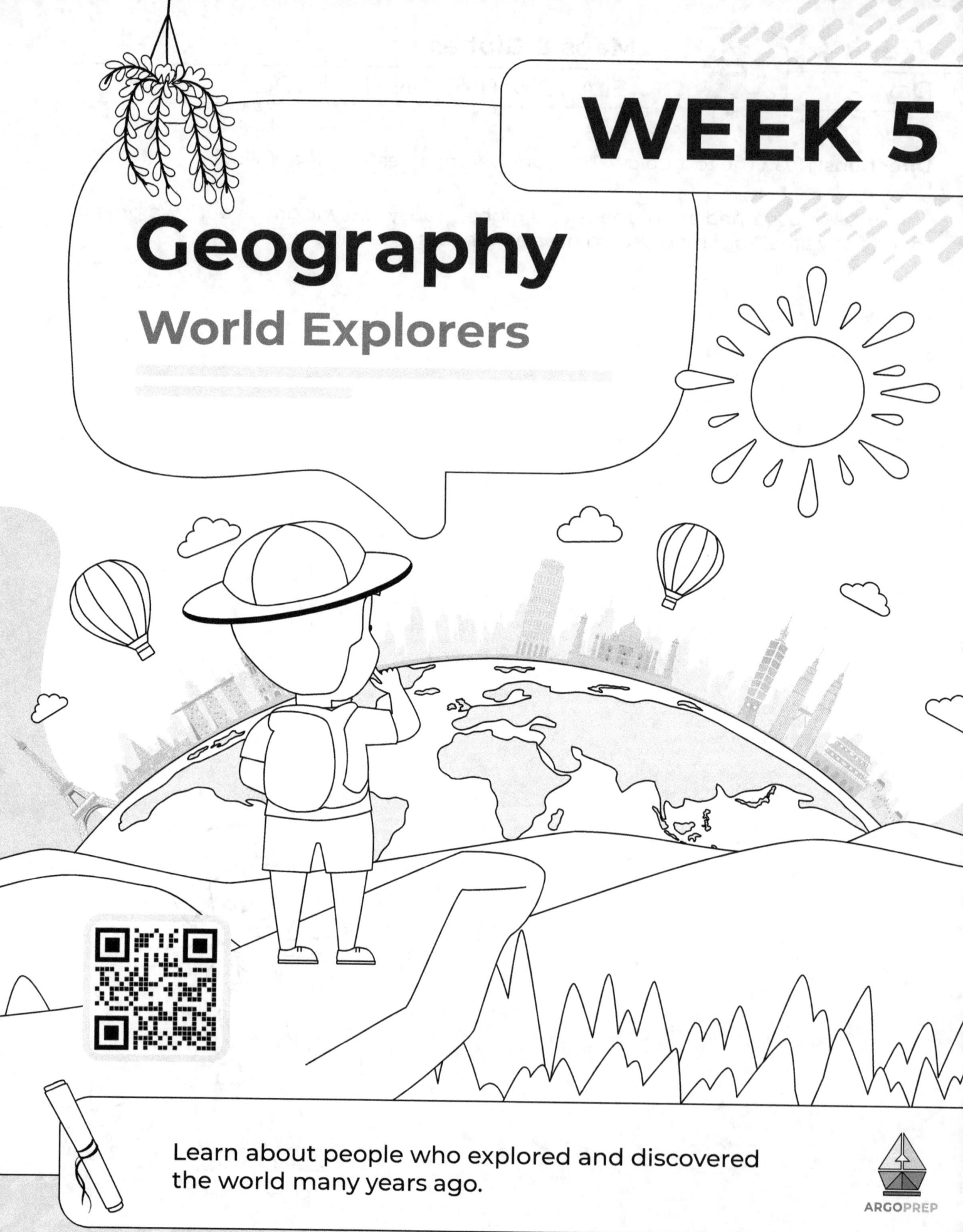

# WEEK 5

# Geography
## World Explorers

Learn about people who explored and discovered the world many years ago.

ARGOPREP

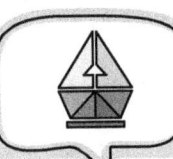
*Last week you learned about maps and globes. You know that people can use them to travel around the world. This week you will learn about famous world explorers.*

**Directions:** Read the text below. Then answer the questions that follow.

Today we have lots of information about the world. But many years ago, people had questions about land and water on Earth. They began to explore to find answers. This started in the 1400s and is known as the **Age of Exploration**. It is also called the Age of Discovery. People began to travel and discover new lands. Some were also looking for treasures like gold and silver.

1. When did people begin to explore the world?

   **A.** in the 1800s

   **B.** in 1776

   **C.** in the 1400s

   **D.** in the past few years

2. The Age of Exploration is also called ............................................. .

   **A.** The Exploration Years

   **B.** The Age of Discovery

   **C.** The Search around the World

   **D.** The Era of World Travel

3. What were world explorers looking for?

   **A.** land

   **B.** treasures

   **C.** information

   **D.** all of these

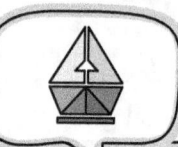
*Yesterday you learned about world explorers. You know early explorers searched the world for land and treasures. Today you will learn more about a famous world explorer.*

**Directions:** Read the text below. Then answer the questions that follow.

> **Ferdinand Magellan** was the first person to travel around the world. He sailed on a boat from Spain to South America in 1519. The boat was named the Trinidad. A crew of sailors came with him on four other boats. On the way, Magellan discovered a passage from the Atlantic Ocean to the Pacific Ocean. It is now called the **Strait of Magellan**. Unfortunately, Magellan died before he could sail back to Spain, but eighteen of his sailors did make it back in 1522. They proved that people could travel around the Earth.

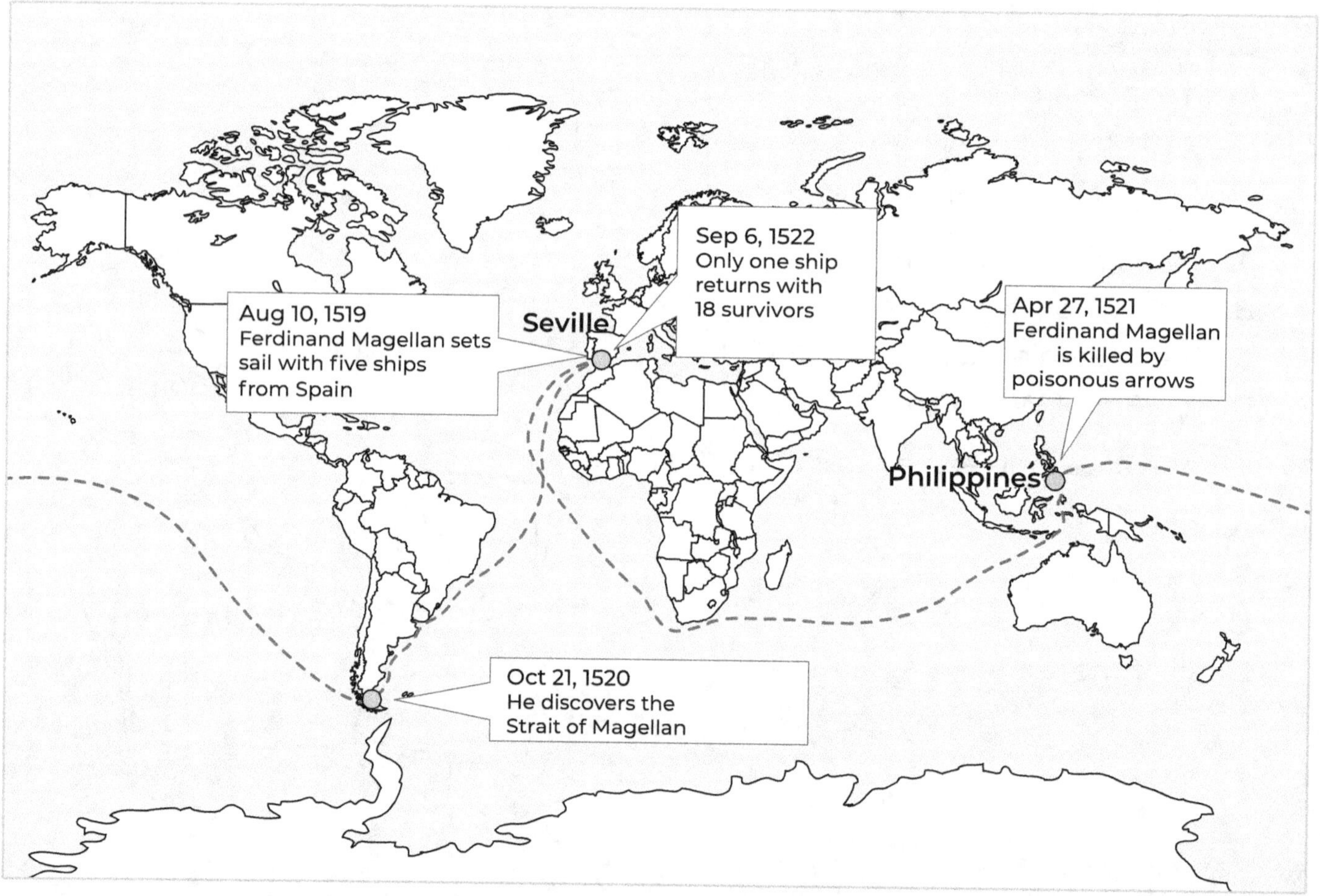

Sep 6, 1522
Only one ship returns with 18 survivors

Aug 10, 1519
Ferdinand Magellan sets sail with five ships from Spain

Seville

Apr 27, 1521
Ferdinand Magellan is killed by poisonous arrows

Philippines

Oct 21, 1520
He discovers the Strait of Magellan

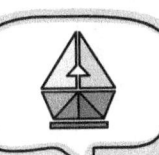
**1.** Ferdinand Magellan was the first person to travel ................................................ .

   **A.** to Spain

   **B.** around the world

   **C.** on a boat

   **D.** from North America

**2.** Magellan discovered a passage we call ................................................ .

   **A.** The Strait of Magellan

   **B.** The Magellan Passage

   **C.** The Route of Magellan

   **D.** Discovery of Magellan

**3.** Only ................................................ of Magellan's sailors made it back to Spain.

   **A.** 32

   **B.** 150

   **C.** 7

   **D.** 18

**4.** True or false?

   It took 3 years to travel around the world.

   **A.** true

   **B.** false

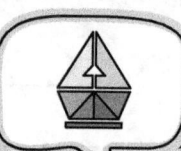
*Yesterday you learned about Ferdinand Magellan, a world explorer. Today you will learn about more world explorers.*

**Directions:** Read the text below. Then answer the questions that follow.

Remember that people traveled the world looking for land and treasures. Many of them made discoveries along the way. Look at the chart below to see what they found.

| World Explorer | Discovery |
| --- | --- |
| **Christopher Columbus** | He traveled from Spain to North America in 1492. He found land which was later colonized by Europeans. This land is now known as America. |
| **Vasco de Gama** | He traveled from Portugal to India in search of spices in 1497. He was the first to make this trip by sea. |
| **Juan Ponce de Leon** | In 1506, he went to the Island of Puerto Rico and discovered gold and land. He was later the first European to explore Florida. |
| **Captain James Cook** | He was known as a great explorer and mapmaker. In 1768, he sailed looking to learn more about astronomy (the study of planets). His observations helped astronomers learn the distance of the Sun from the Earth. |

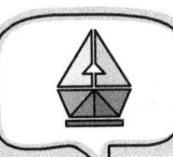
**1.** Did Juan Ponce de Leon find treasures or land?

........................................................................................................................

........................................................................................................................

........................................................................................................................

**2.** How did Captain James Cook's discoveries help astronomers?

........................................................................................................................

........................................................................................................................

........................................................................................................................

**3.** Which of these 4 explorers is most interesting to you and why?

........................................................................................................................

........................................................................................................................

........................................................................................................................

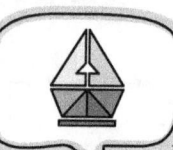
**Directions:** Read the text below. Then answer the questions that follow.

Imagine you are a world explorer. Where would you go? What would you search for? Today you will plan your trip. Write these details below.

## My World Exploration Trip

Where will I go?

........................................................................................

How will I get there?

........................................................................................

How long will the trip take?

........................................................................................

What will I search for?

........................................................................................

What do I expect to find?

........................................................................................

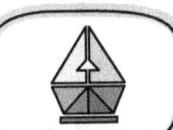
*This week you learned about world explorers. Today you will review what you have learned.*

**1.** What was the name of Magellan's boat?

   **A.** The Trinidad

   **B.** The Amazon

   **C.** The Explorer

   **D.** The Magellan

**2.** What was Vasco de Gama looking for when he went to India?

   **A.** silver

   **B.** animals

   **C.** islands

   **D.** spices

**3.** Who was the first European to explore Florida?

   **A.** Christopher Columbus

   **B.** Juan Ponce de Leon

   **C.** Captain James Cook

   **D.** Vasco de Gama

**4.** Christopher Columbus traveled from Spain to ............................................. .

   **A.** South America

   **B.** Australia

   **C.** North America

   **D.** Africa

# WEEK 6

# History
## World Settlers

Learn about the first Europeans settlers in America.

ARGOPREP

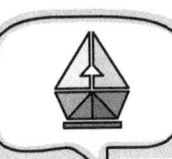
*Last week you learned about world explorers. You know people traveled the world in search of land and treasures. Some explorers were also looking for a new life in a new land. They were called **settlers**.*

**Directions:** Read the text below. Then answer the questions that follow.

> Many settlers came from Europe. They wanted to find new land for different reasons. Some of them believed they could make more money. New land would be better for growing and selling crops. Some settlers did not want to have rulers, such as kings. If they found their own land, they could make their own rules.

**1.** Who are settlers?

    **A.** people who have lived in the same place for a long time

    **B.** people who start a new life in a new place

    **C.** people who like to travel to new places for a short visit

    **D.** people who search the world for treasures

**2.** Many settlers came from ........................................ .

    **A.** New Jersey

    **B.** Europe

    **C.** Antarctica

    **D.** none of these places

**3.** Why did settlers want to find new land?

    **A.** to make more money

    **B.** to grow and sell crops

    **C.** to make their own rules

    **D.** all of these reasons

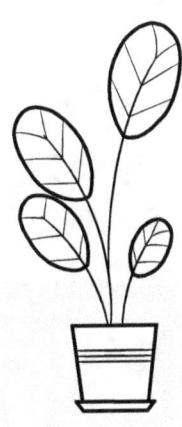

*Yesterday you learned about settlers. You know European settlers wanted a new life in a new land. Today you will learn about settlers who came to America.*

**Directions:** Read the text below. Then answer the questions that follow.

Remember that Christopher Columbus came to North America in 1492. He and his crew sailed on three ships: the Niña, the Pinta and the Santa Maria. Columbus was looking for a way to travel from Europe to Asia by water. He was also looking for treasures such as gems, gold and spices. On the way, he learned there was land on the other side of the Earth. There were people living on the land who we now call Native Americans. But many Euorpeans had never seen or heard of this land. It was an amazing discovery.

Many years later, in the 1600s, settlers came to North America. They began to form **colonies**. A colony is a group of people who settle in a new place. The first American colony was founded in Jamestown, Virginia. This was the beginning of America.

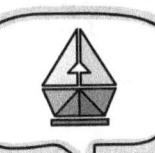
1. Columbus and his crew sailed on three ships: the Niña, the Pinta and the ............................................. .

    A. Trinidad

    B. Atlantic

    C. Santa Maria

    D. Spain

2. What was Columbus looking for?

    A. a travel route from Europe to Asia

    B. gems, gold and spices

    C. both A and B

    D. none of these

3. A ............................................. is a group of people who settle in a new place.

    A. colony

    B. explorer

    C. tourist

    D. country

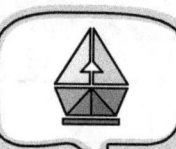
*Yesterday you learned about how America began.*

**Directions:** Read the text below. Then answer the questions that follow.

" You know European settlers started American colonies in the 1600s. The first colony was founded in Jamestown, Virginia in 1607. By the 1700s, there were 13 American colonies. Georgia was the last colony, founded in 1732. These colonies were divided into 3 regions: New England colonies, Middle colonies and Southern colonies.

People lived different lives in each region. New England colonies were good areas for farming, fishing and hunting. Middle colonies were known for **exporting goods** (selling and sending them to people in other places) such as wheat and other grains. Southern colonies had fertile land which was good for growing crops and raising farm animals. "

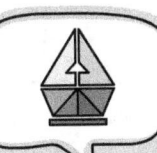
1.  Which of these colonies was located in the Southern region?

    **A.** Maine

    **B.** New York

    **C.** Georgia

    **D.** Pennsylvania

2.  In what region was New Hampshire located?

    **A.** New England

    **B.** Middle

    **C.** Southern

    **D.** all of these regions

3.  Which of these colonies was known for exporting grains?

    **A.** New England

    **B.** Middle

    **C.** Southern

    **D.** none of these regions

4.  Explain how people lived different lives in the 3 colony regions.

    ..................................................................................................................................

    ..................................................................................................................................

    ..................................................................................................................................

    ..................................................................................................................................

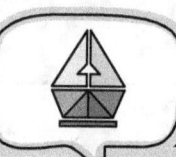
**Directions:** Read the text below. Then answer the questions that follow.

Remember that settlers came from Europe to America many years ago. Today you will think about how people lived in colonial times. Look at the table below. How is life different in America now? Write your answers in the column on the right.

| Colonial Times | America Today |
|---|---|
| only 13 colonies (later became states) | |
| people hunted and grew their own food | |
| people used fire to cook food | |
| people lived in homes made from wood, mud and grass | |
| people traveled by horses and wagons | |

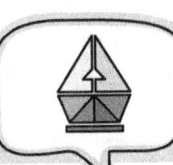
**Directions:** Read the text below. Then answer the questions that follow.

This week you learned about early American settlers. Today you will create a timeline of events based on what you learned from the reading in Day 2 and Day 3.

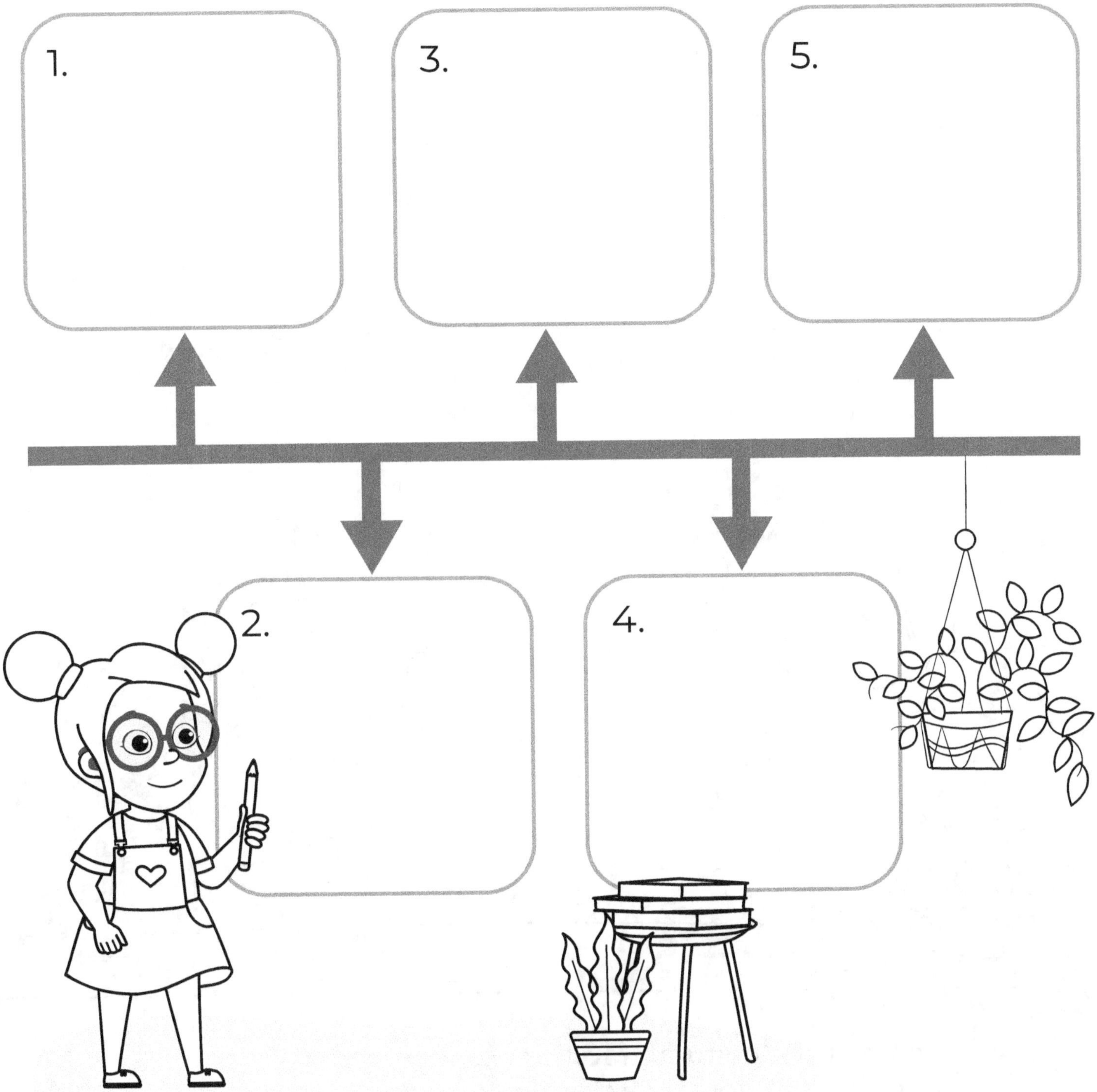

1.

3.

5.

2.

4.

# WEEK 7

# History

## Cultures & Traditions: Past and Present

Learn about cultural traditions/celebrations and find out how they started.

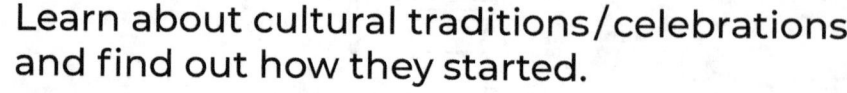

ARGOPREP

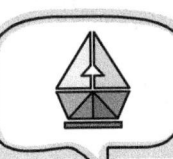
*Last week you learned about world settlers. You know people traveled from Europe to America to start a new life. This week you will learn about American culture and traditions.*

**Directions:** Read the text below. Then answer the questions that follow.

**Culture** is the way people live. It is the way people eat, dress, believe and celebrate. Remember that life was different for Americans during colonial times. That is because culture can change over time. Americans do not live the same way they did many years ago. However, **traditions** do not change. This part of culture is passed down for many years. For example, people started celebrating Independence Day in the 1700s. This is a traditional American holiday that people still celebrate.

1. What is culture?

   **A.** the way people live

   **B.** the number of people living in a place

   **C.** settlers living in new land

   **D.** people who lived many years ago

2. Which of these is NOT a part of culture?

   **A.** food

   **B.** clothing

   **C.** celebrations

   **D.** age

3. True or false?

   American traditions change once every year.

   **A.** true

   **B.** false

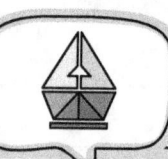
*You know culture is the way people live. Culture changes over time. Traditions stay the same for many years. Today you will learn about American traditions.*

**Directions:** Read the text below. Then answer the questions that follow.

Remember that settlers came to America from Europe. Some American traditions have **origins** in Europe. An origin is where something begins. American traditions may also come from important events during colonial times. Look at the table below. It shows traditional **holidays**, or special yearly celebrations, in America.

| Holiday | Origin | Celebrations Today |
| --- | --- | --- |
| **St. Patrick's Day** | The first St. Patrick's feast took place in Ireland many years ago in the 400s. It was a day to celebrate a man whom many believed was a hero. People told stories about how St. Patrick drove out all the snakes from Ireland. He was also known for carrying a shamrock. | People in America have St. Patrick's Day parades on March 17th every year. They often wear green clothing and have feasts with corned beef and cabbage. The shamrock is a symbol of St. Patrick's Day. |
| **Independence Day (Fourth of July)** | The first Independence Day was July 4, 1776. On this day, America became independent from British rulers. Americans celebrated with bells, music, and parades. Later celebrations included fireworks and bonfires. | Americans still celebrate Independence Day on July 4th. People have picnics and parades with food and fireworks. They wear the colors red, white and blue. |
| **Thanksgiving Day** | In 1621, American settlers and Native Americans had an autumn harvest feast. Native Americans taught the settlers how to grow crops. They gathered food such as meat, corn, fish, berries and pumpkins. This was known as the first Thanksgiving. | Americans celebrate Thanksgiving on the fourth Thursday of November. They eat large feasts with food such as turkey, potatoes, corn, cranberries and pumpkin pie. |

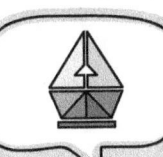
**1.** Compare and contrast a tradition from the table. How has it changed over the years? How has it stayed the same?

.......................................................................................................................

.......................................................................................................................

.......................................................................................................................

.......................................................................................................................

.......................................................................................................................

**2.** Explain how American traditions were started by European settlers.

.......................................................................................................................

.......................................................................................................................

.......................................................................................................................

.......................................................................................................................

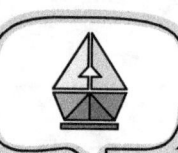
*Yesterday you learned about traditions and holidays. These celebrations are an important part of culture.* **Symbols** *are also part of culture and traditions. A symbol is a picture or object that stands for something else. The American flag, for example, is an important symbol that represents freedom. Today you will learn about flags around the world.*

**Directions:** Read the text below. Then answer the questions that follow.

> There are nearly 200 country flags in the world! Each flag is a special symbol for its country. They all have different colors or pictures. The American flag is red, white and blue. It has 50 stars and 13 stripes. The United Kingdom's flag is also red, white and blue. It has lines that cross each other like the letter "x" with a cross in the center. The flag of Canada is red and white with a maple leaf in the middle. The maple leaf is a Canadian symbol of unity and peace. The flag of Japan is also red and white. It has a red circle in the middle of a white background.

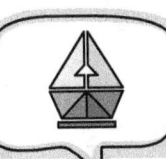
Look at each flag below. Write the country that it belongs to on the line.

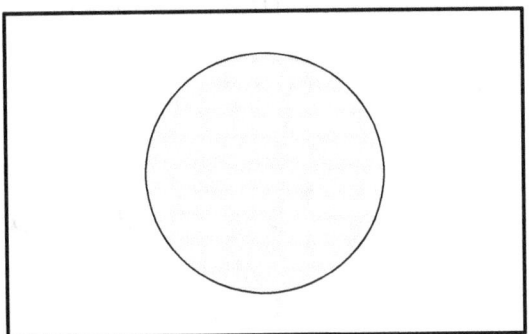

**1.** .................................................

**2.** .................................................

**3.** .................................................

**4.** .................................................

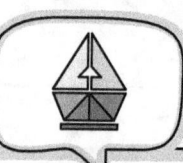
*You know traditions are an important part of culture. Today you will think about your own culture. What are some traditions in your family?*

**Directions:** Read the text below. Then answer the questions that follow.

Draw or paste pictures in the boxes below.

| My Culture & Traditions | |
|---|---|
| **food** | **clothing** |
| **flag** | **celebrations** |

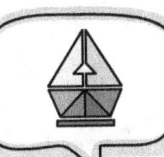
**Directions:** Read the text below. Then answer the questions that follow.

This week you learned about culture and traditions. Today you will review what you have learned.

1. Which of these is a holiday tradition?

   A. going to a St. Patrick's Day parade
   B. having a Thanksgiving feast
   C. watching a fireworks show on the Fourth of July
   D. all of these

2. A(n) ............................... is where a tradition begins.

   A. symbol
   B. origin
   C. holiday
   D. culture

3. The flag of ............................... is red and white with a maple leaf in the middle.

   A. Canada
   B. the United States of America
   C. Japan
   D. the United Kingdom

4. Which of these is a symbol?

   A. France
   B. a picnic
   C. a shamrock
   D. an origin

# WEEK 8

# History

## Arts, Music & Dance

Explore traditional art, music and dance from various cultures around the world.

ARGOPREP

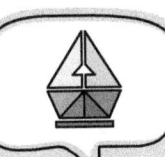
*Last week you learned about culture. Cultural traditions are passed down over the years. Remember that food, clothing and celebrations are part of culture. This week you will learn about more traditions such as art, music and dance.*

**Directions:** Read the text below. Then answer the questions that follow.

Art is an important part of culture. People create art such as paintings, pottery and sculptures all over the world. Sometimes these creations are saved for many years. They are used as **artifacts**. An artifact is something which was made by someone of a specific culture in the past. It is used to learn more about the history of that culture.

1. Which of these is an example of art?

    **A.** feasts

    **B.** pottery

    **C.** hunting

    **D.** shoes

2. What is an artifact?

    **A.** something that was made by someone of a specific culture

    **B.** someone who has created art for many years

    **C.** something that is celebrated once a year

    **D.** someone who studies the history of art

3. Which of these is an artifact?

    **A.** a man who has lived in Mexico for many years

    **B.** a family who eats a traditional Mexican dinner every year

    **C.** a painting that was created in Mexico 50 years ago

    **D.** an explorer who traveled to Mexico in the 1600s

4. How can artifacts help people learn about history?

    ...................................................................................................................................

    ...................................................................................................................................

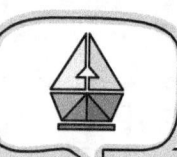
*Yesterday you learned about artifacts. You know artifacts help people learn about culture and history. Today you will learn about artifacts from Mayan culture.*

**Directions:** Read the text below. Then answer the questions that follow.

"

Mayan civilization started many years ago during **ancient** times. Scientists have found many Mayan artifacts. Some of them were made over 1,000 years ago. The Maya people are known for their unique sculptures. These sculptures were carved from materials such as wood, bone and clay. Mayans also used paint made from plants and clay to create colorful wall paintings. The paintings told stories about the Maya people. Mayan masks were made from stones and gems. These masks were worn by Mayan rulers during celebrations. Mayan pottery was carved out of clay and decorated. People used these pottery pieces as bowls and vases.

"

**1.** Some Mayan artifacts were made ................................. years ago.

   **A.** just a few

   **B.** about 10

   **C.** less than 100

   **D.** over 1,000

**2.** What are ancient times?

   **A.** a time period that happened many years ago

   **B.** the time period that we live in today

   **C.** a time period that will happen in the future

   **D.** an unknown time period

**3.** What were Mayan sculptures made from?

   **A.** bone

   **B.** clay

   **C.** wood

   **D.** all of these

**4.** The Maya people used ............................. to tell stories.

   **A.** television

   **B.** paintings

   **C.** books

   **D.** all of these

**5.** Who wore Mayan masks?

   **A.** Mayan children

   **B.** Mayan women

   **C.** Mayan rulers

   **D.** all Maya people

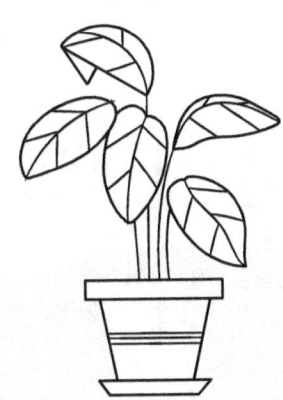

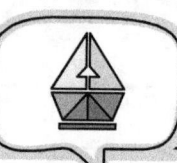
**Directions:** Read the text below. Then answer the questions that follow.

You know art is an important part of culture and history. Artifacts can be used to learn about how people lived in the past. Music and dance can also be cultural traditions. Today you will learn about different types of traditional music. Look at the table below.

| Music | Origin |
|---|---|
| **salsa** | Salsa music began in Latin American countries such as Cuba and Mexico. Salsa dancers wear colorful costumes and play instruments such as maracas and guitars. |
| **opera** | Opera music started in Italy in the late 1500s. It combines singing, dancing, and stage plays. |
| **country** | The southern part of the United States is known for country music. It became popular in the 1900s. People sing and play instruments such as fiddles, banjos and guitars. |
| **reggae** | Reggae started in the country of Jamaica in the 1960s. It has sounds of drums, bass guitars and Jamaican stick instruments. |
| **folk** | People tell stories through folk music. It started in Europe. There are different types of folk music. Scottish folk music is played at celebrations with bagpipes and fiddles. Pandavani is a popular type of folk music in India. |

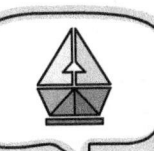
**1.** Salsa music is traditional in ........................................ countries.

   **A.** Chinese

   **B.** Canadian

   **C.** Australian

   **D.** Latin American

**2.** Where did opera music begin?

   **A.** Africa

   **B.** New York

   **C.** Italy

   **D.** Cuba

**3.** Which of these instruments is played in country music?

   **A.** maracas

   **B.** banjo

   **C.** Jamaican stick instruments

   **D.** all of these

**4.** How do people use music to tell stories?

........................................................................................................

........................................................................................................

........................................................................................................

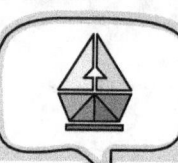
*Yesterday you learned about traditional music. Today you will answer a few questions about music in your own culture.*

**Directions:** Read the text below. Then answer the questions that follow.

1. What kind of music traditions does your family have? Where does this music come from?

   ................................................................................................

   ................................................................................................

   ................................................................................................

2. What is your favorite traditional song and why?

   ................................................................................................

   ................................................................................................

   ................................................................................................

3. How is dance a part of your family traditions?

   ................................................................................................

   ................................................................................................

   ................................................................................................

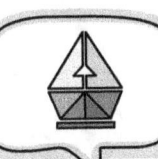
**Directions:** Read the text below. Then answer the questions that follow.

This week you learned about traditional art, music and dance. Today you will use resources (books, Internet, etc.). to learn about The Harlem Renaissance. Write what you learned about art, music, and dance from this famous time period.

| The Harlem Renaissance | |
|---|---|
| **art** | |
| **music** | |
| **dance** | |

# WEEK 9

# History

## Folktales

Explore traditional folktales and learn about their origins.

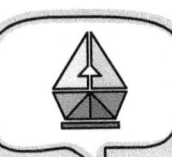
*You know people tell stories through art, music and dance. This week you will learn about **folktales**. Folktales are stories that are told for many years. They are passed down through generations.*

**Directions:** Read the text below. Then answer the questions that follow.

"Many years ago there were no books. People did not write stories down. They told them over and over so people would remember them. Years later, people began to write stories. They remembered the old folktales that were once told. That is how people are able to read them today.

1. What are folktales?

    A. books that were written many years ago
    B. stories that were told many years ago
    C. new stories that are told about the past
    D. people who like to tell old stories

2. How were folktales passed down over the years?

    A. people wrote them down
    B. people changed them into new stories
    C. people told them over and over again
    D. people forgot about them over the years

3. True or false?

    Folktales are no longer available for people to read.

    A. true
    B. false

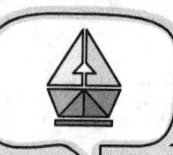
*Yesterday you learned about folktales. You know folktales are stories that are told for many years. Today you will read a Native American folktale. Remember that Native Americans lived in North America long before the settlers came. They often told stories about their culture.*

**Directions:** Read the text below. Then answer the questions that follow.

## Why the Owl Has Big Eyes

an Iroquois folktale (adapted)

Raweno, the Maker of Everything, was busy creating animals. He was working on Rabbit. Rabbit said, "I want long legs and ears like a deer. I want sharp fangs and claws like a panther."

"I will give you what you ask for," said Raweno. He made Rabbit's long hind legs.

Owl was sitting on a tree waiting for his turn. He said, "Whoo, whoo, I want a long neck like a swan. I want beautiful red feathers like a cardinal. I want a crown of feathers like a heron. I want you to make me the most beautiful of all the birds."

Raweno said, "Be quiet! Turn around and look away. Even better, just close your eyes. No one is allowed to watch me work." Then Raweno made Rabbit's long ears just as he had asked.

Owl refused to do what Raweno said. "Whoo, whoo," he replied, "Nobody can forbid me to watch. Nobody can order me to close my eyes. I like watching you, and I will keep watching."

Raweno became angry. He grabbed Owl, pulling him down from his branch. He stuffed his head deep into his body. He shook him until his eyes grew big with fright. He pulled Owl's ears until they were sticking up on both sides of his head.

"There," said Raweno. "That will teach you. Now you won't be able to stretch your neck. You will not watch things that you shouldn't see. Now you have big ears to listen. Use them when someone tells you what not to do. Now you have big eyes. You will awake only at night. You will not be able to see me when I work in the morning. Your feathers won't be red like a cardinal. They will be gray because you did not obey." Raweno rubbed gray mud all over Owl's feathers.

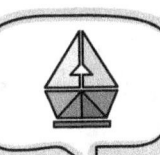
"

So Owl flew off pouting and crying, "Whoo, whoo, whoo."

Then Raweno turned back to finish making Rabbit. But Rabbit had seen Raweno's anger. He was so afraid that he hopped away unfinished. As a result, Rabbit's hind legs are long. His front legs are short. He has to hop around instead of walking and running. Also, he never got the claws and fangs he asked for. Had he not run away, Rabbit would have been a stronger, faster animal.

As for Owl, he stayed the way Raweno made him. He has big eyes and a short neck. He has ears sticking up on the sides of his head. Worst of all, he has to sleep all day and come out only at night.

"

**1.** Folktales are often told to teach lessons. What lessons can you learn from this story?

..................................................................................................................................................

..................................................................................................................................................

..................................................................................................................................................

**2.** What can you learn about Native American culture from this story?

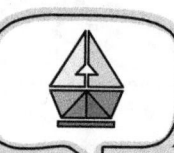
*Yesterday you read a Native American folktale. You know folktales are important in this culture. Folktales are told all over the world. Today you will learn about folktales from various cultures.*

**Directions:** Read the text below. Then answer the questions that follow.

Some folktales were told in one place and then spread to other places. The whole story did not change, but people made it different to fit their culture. Some characters' names were changed. Some words were changed to a different language.

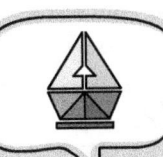
You may have heard the story of Little Red Riding Hood. It is a popular folktale from Europe. This story is also told in many other countries. Use resources to find other versions of Little Red Riding Hood. Write the title and the country that it is from in the table below.

| country | title |
|---------|-------|
|         |       |
|         |       |
|         |       |

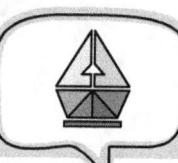
**Directions:** Read the text below. Then answer the questions that follow.

Remember that folktales were told many years ago. Today we can read them in books. What is your favorite folktale? Write about it below.

## My Favorite Folktale

**Title:** ............................................................................................................

**Origin:** ............................................................................................................

**Characters:** ............................................................................................................

**Summary:** ............................................................................................................

............................................................................................................

............................................................................................................

............................................................................................................

............................................................................................................

............................................................................................................

............................................................................................................

............................................................................................................

............................................................................................................

............................................................................................................

**Directions:** Read the text below. Then answer the questions that follow.

This week you learned about folktales and culture. Today you will review what you have learned.

**1.** Which of the following is <u>NOT</u> true about folktales?

    **A.** The titles may change in different cultures.

    **B.** The characters may be different in another country.

    **C.** Some folktales have many different versions.

    **D.** Folktales must always remain exactly the same.

**2.** *Why the Owl Has Big Eyes* is a ........................................ folktale.

    **A.** Native American

    **B.** Chinese

    **C.** Spanish

    **D.** French

**3.** Why do people tell folktales?

    **A.** to share old stories

    **B.** to teach about culture

    **C.** to teach lessons

    **D.** all of these reasons

# WEEK 10

# History
## World Languages

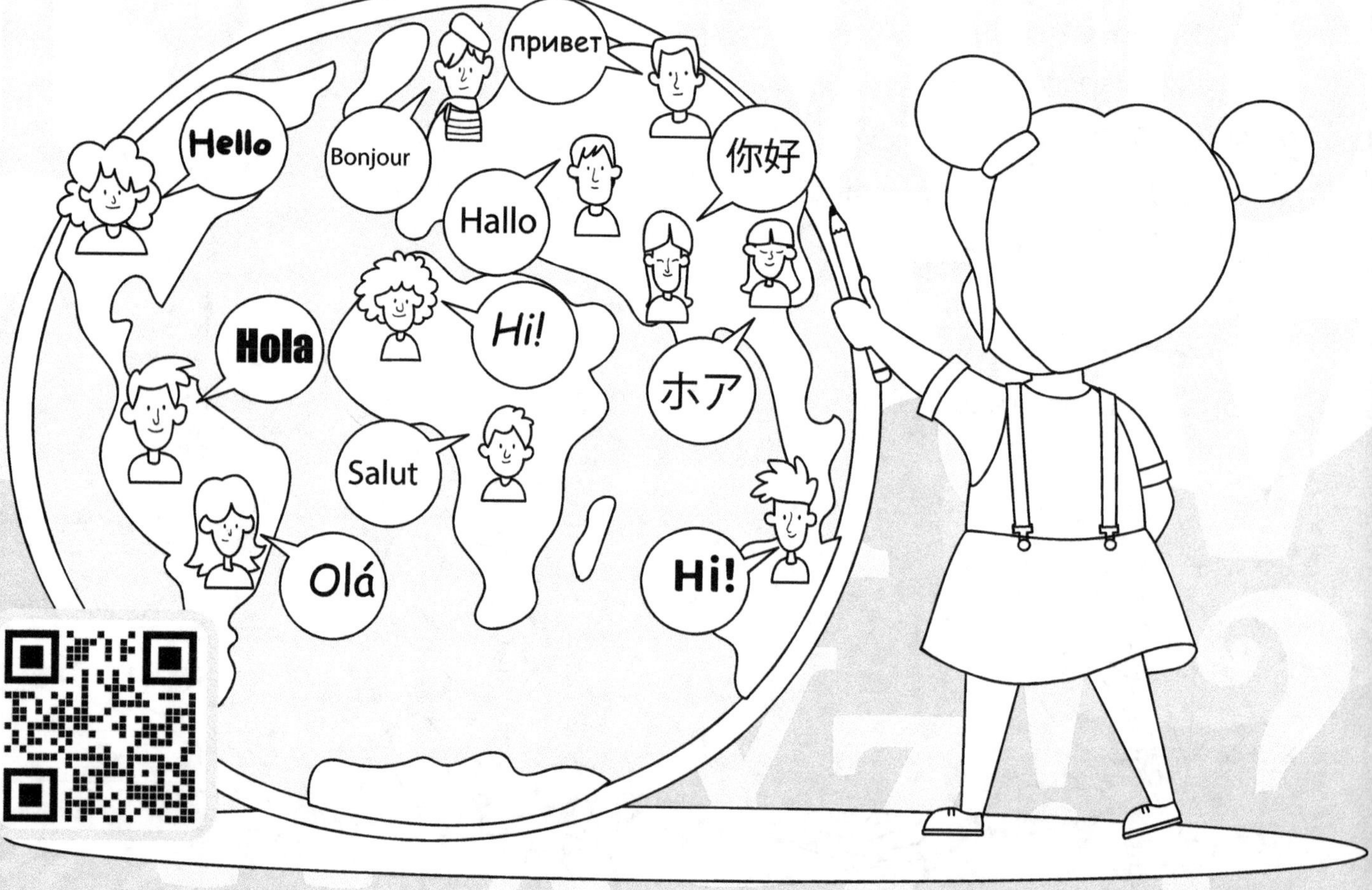

Discover many ways to communicate around the world.

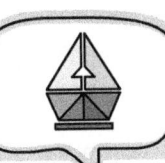
*Last week you learned about folktales. Remember that the same story can have different titles around the world. This is because people speak different **languages**. Language is the way people communicate. People use language to talk and write.*

**Directions:** Read the text below. Then answer the questions that follow.

> There are over 6,000 languages spoken around the world. Some countries have one main language. Most or all of the people who live there speak this language. Other countries have many languages. For example, there are more than 500 languages spoken in the African country of Nigeria.

**1.** Language is the way people .................................... .

   **A.** live

   **B.** travel

   **C.** communicate

   **D.** celebrate

**2.** There are over ............................ languages spoken around the world.

   **A.** 500,000

   **B.** 6,000

   **C.** 70,000

   **D.** 4,000,000

**3.** How do people use language?

   **A.** to talk to one another

   **B.** to write letters

   **C.** both A and B

   **D.** none of these

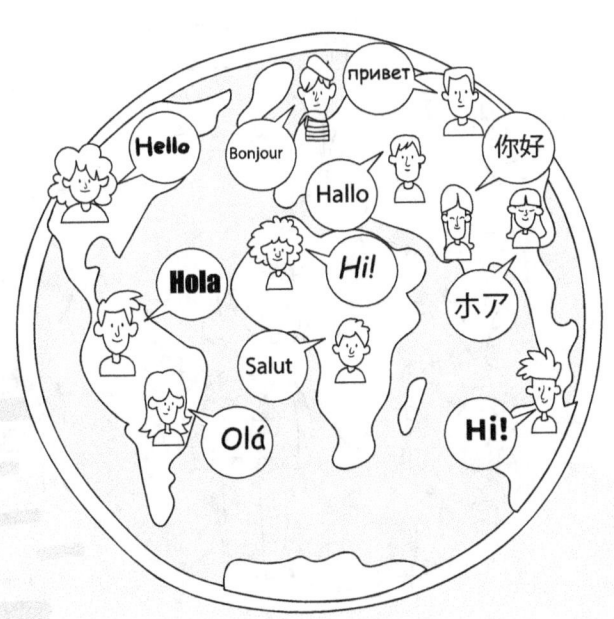

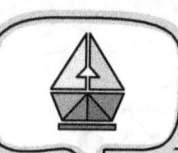
*Yesterday you learned about world languages. People use language to communicate. Today you will learn about why language is important.*

**Directions:** Read the text below. Then answer the questions that follow.

> What if there were no languages in the world? People might use their hands to communicate. They could draw pictures. They might even make expressions with their faces. This is called **non-verbal communication**. It is a way to communicate without words. While this is possible, spoken language helps people express themselves much more easily.
>
> People also need languages in order to write. There are many different **writing systems** in the world. People use letters or symbols to write language. These writing systems are not all the same. The English language uses an **alphabet**. Each letter in the alphabet makes a sound. These letters are put together to write words. Languages such as Chinese use symbols. The symbols have special meanings and sounds.

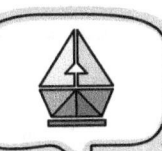
1. Which of these is an example of non-verbal communication?

   A. talking to your neighbor

   B. reading a story aloud

   C. smiling at a friend

   D. saying "hello" to your teacher

2. What are writing systems?

   A. a system that uses letters or sounds to write language

   B. a system that uses cell phones to communicate

   C. a system that does not use words to communicate

   D. all of these

3. True or false?

   Writing systems are not all the same.

   A. true

   B. false

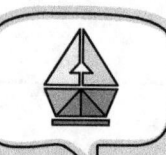
*Yesterday you learned about why language is important. People need language to express and write words. Language also helps people connect with others.*

**Directions:** Read the text below. Then answer the questions that follow.

Have you ever greeted a stranger? What do you say when a friend does something nice for you? There are many ways to say "hello" and "thank you." Today, you will learn how to say these words in different languages. Use resources to help you find the answers. Write them in the chart below.

| language | "hello" | "thank you" |
|---|---|---|
| Spanish | | |
| French | | |
| Italian | | |

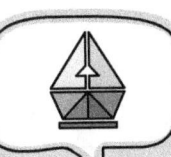
| language | "hello" | "thank you" |
|---|---|---|
| Chinese |  |  |
| Swahili |  |  |

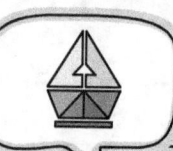
**Directions:** Read the text below. Then answer the questions that follow.

You know there are many different world languages. Today you will think about languages in your family and community.

**1.** What language (or languages) do you speak at home?

.......................................................................................................................

.......................................................................................................................

.......................................................................................................................

**2.** Do you speak a different language at school? Explain.

.......................................................................................................................

.......................................................................................................................

.......................................................................................................................

**3.** If you could learn a new language, what would it be?

.......................................................................................................................

.......................................................................................................................

.......................................................................................................................

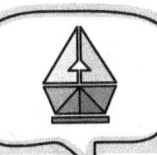
**Directions:** Read the text below. Then answer the questions that follow.

This week you learned about world languages. Today you will answer a few more questions about what you learned.

1. ............................................ is when people communicate without words.

   **A.** Writing systems

   **B.** Non-verbal communication

   **C.** Language

   **D.** Storytelling

2. The English language is written with ............................................ .

   **A.** pictures

   **B.** numbers

   **C.** letters

   **D.** symbols

3. True or false?

   Every country has one main language.

   **A.** true

   **B.** false

4. Name 3 ways to say "hello" around the world.

   ............................................................................

   ............................................................................

   ............................................................................

# WEEK 11

## Civics & Government
### World Leaders

Learn about various types of leaders around the world.

ARGOPREP

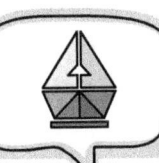
*You have learned about world communities. You know there are many large and small communities on Earth. This week you will learn about world leaders.*

**Directions:** Read the text below. Then answer the questions that follow.

Think about communities such as cities, states and countries. Each of them has a special leadership system. This system is called the **government**. Government leaders have the power to make important decisions for community **citizens**. A citizen is a person who lives in a specific place.

Local government includes leaders such as mayors and governors. Mayors lead cities and towns, while governors lead states. National government leaders, such as presidents, lead countries.

**1.** What is the government?

    **A.** someone who lives in a specific community

    **B.** a leadership system that makes community decisions

    **C.** a small community that does not have a leader

    **D.** a citizen who moves to a new community

**2.** Which of these is a national government leader?

    **A.** mayor

    **B.** governor

    **C.** principal

    **D.** president

**3.** True or false?

Small communities, such as towns, do not have a government.

    **A.** true

    **B.** false

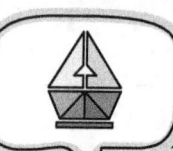
*Yesterday you learned about government leaders. You know they have the power to lead both large and small communities. Mayors lead cities, for example. Countries are led by presidents. There are other types of national leaders. Today you will learn about them.*

**Directions:** Read the text below. Then answer the questions that follow.

Countries such as India and Canada have a **prime minister**. Like a president, the prime minister leads the country and makes important decisions. The United Kingdom is led by a prime minister. This country also has a **king** or **queen** as a leader. They work together with the prime minister.

Kings and queens may be part of a **dynasty**. This is when leaders come from the same family. This was also common for Chinese **emperors** many years ago. When the emperor died, his son became the new emperor.

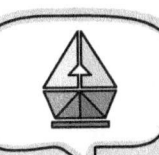
**1.** The country of India is led by a ........................................ .

    **A.** president

    **B.** queen

    **C.** prime minister

    **D.** governor

**2.** A dynasty is when leaders come from the same ........................................ .

    **A.** government

    **B.** country

    **C.** family

    **D.** neighborhood

**3.** When a Chinese emperor died, his ........................................ became the new leader.

    **A.** son

    **B.** queen

    **C.** father

    **D.** mayor

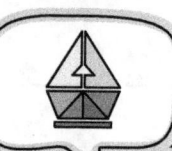
*You know countries can be led by different types of leaders. Today you will learn about a few famous world leaders.*

**Directions:** Read the text below. Then answer the questions that follow.

Look at the table below. On the left, there is the name of a world leader. Use resources to find out what type of leader they are and which country they lead. Write what you learned in the column on the right.

| World Leader | Title/Country |
|---|---|
| **Queen Elizabeth II** | |
| **Narendra Modi** | |

| World Leader | Title/Country |
|---|---|
| **Xi Jinping** | |
| **Sergio Mattarella** | |

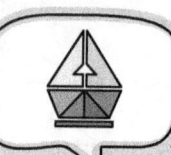
**Directions:** Read the text below. Then answer the questions that follow.

Yesterday you learned about famous world leaders. Today you will learn more about your own national leader. What country do you live in? Use resources to find out who the leader is. Write what you learned below.

I live in the country of ................................................................ .
*(leader's name)*

is the ........................................................................ of my country. Here are a few fun facts
*(type of leader)*

about .................................................................. .
*(leader's name)*

1. ................................................................................................................................

................................................................................................................................

................................................................................................................................

2. ................................................................................................................................

................................................................................................................................

................................................................................................................................

3. ................................................................................................................................

................................................................................................................................

................................................................................................................................

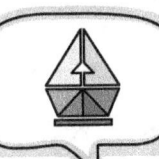
**Directions:** Read the text below. Then answer the questions that follow.

You have learned about world leaders this week. Today you will answer a few more questions about what you have learned.

1. Which of these is NOT a national government leader?

   **A.** mayor

   **B.** president

   **C.** prime minister

   **D.** king

2. Which of these countries is led by a prime minister?

   **A.** The United States of America

   **B.** Canada

   **C.** Italy

   **D.** none of these

3. The Chinese emperor Hongwu died in 1398. His grandson, Jianwen, became the new emperor. What is this called?

   **A.** a dynasty

   **B.** a citizen

   **C.** a governor

   **D.** all of these

4. Explain how both small and large communities can have government leaders.

   _____

   _____

   _____

# WEEK 12

## Civics & Government

### Laws

Learn about community laws and why they are important.

ARGOPREP

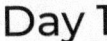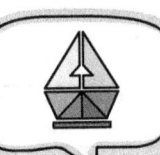
*Last week you learned about government leaders. You know they lead communities and make important decisions. Government leaders also make* **laws**, *or a system of rules. Part of their job is to make sure that people follow them.*

**Directions:** Read the text below. Then answer the questions that follow.

> Laws are important for quite a few reasons. First, they keep people safe. Imagine if there were no traffic laws. Drivers would be more likely to harm themselves and others. Laws also protect property. People cannot take whatever they want from others. If someone does break the law, there are consequences. They could be charged a **fine** or sent to jail. A fine is an amount of money that people must pay for their crimes.

**1.** Government leaders make a system of ................................................ called laws.

    **A.** communities

    **B.** money

    **C.** rules

    **D.** fines

**2.** Why are laws important?

    **A.** They keep people safe.

    **B.** They make roads safer for drivers.

    **C.** They protect property.

    **D.** all of these reasons

**3.** What is a fine?

    **A.** a place where people go if they commit a crime

    **B.** an amount of money that people must pay for their crimes

    **C.** a type of law that people must follow

    **D.** a community that does not follow any laws

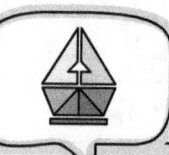
*Yesterday you learned about laws. You know government leaders make laws. They also make sure that people follow them. Today you will learn more about the lawmaking process.*

**Directions:** Read the text below. Then answer the questions that follow.

> A law starts as an idea. It is turned into a bill for **Congress** to vote on. Congress is a group of leaders who make laws. In America, Congress has two parts: the Senate and the House of Representatives. Both parts must agree on a bill. If they do, it is sent to the President who can sign the bill and make it a law or **veto** it. When a bill is vetoed, it is rejected and does not become a law.

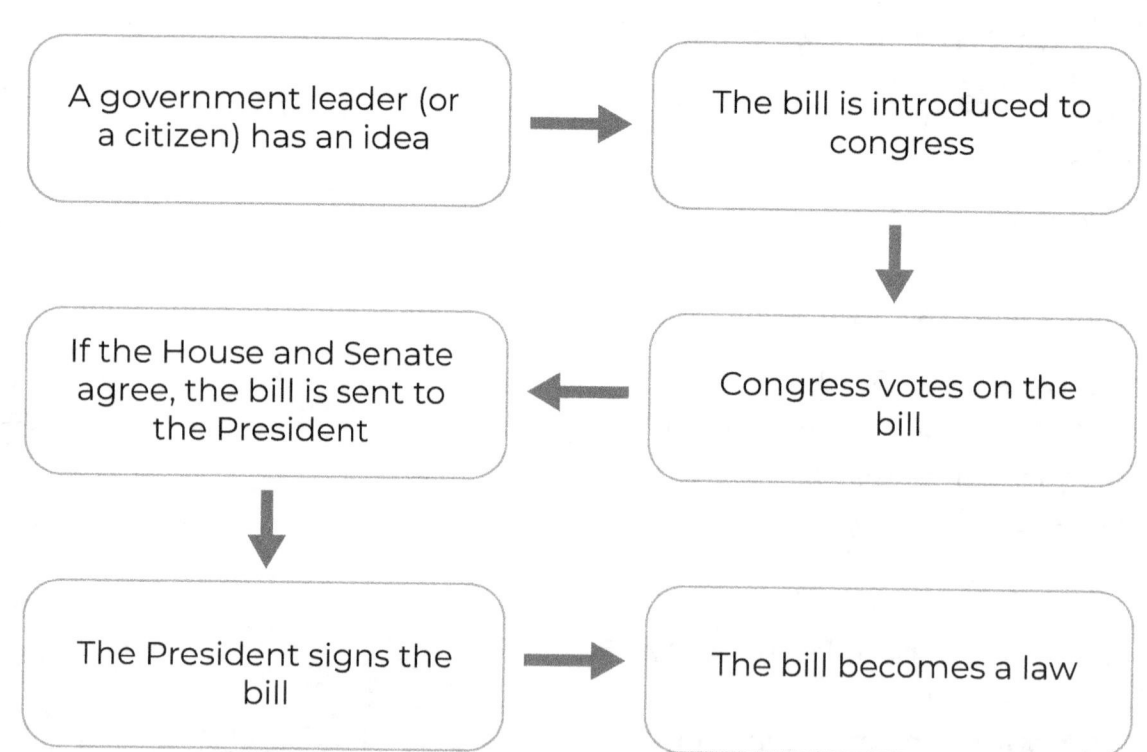

A government leader (or a citizen) has an idea → The bill is introduced to congress

Congress votes on the bill → If the House and Senate agree, the bill is sent to the President

The President signs the bill → The bill becomes a law

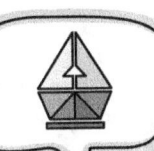
**1.** Which of these steps happens first?

   **A.** Someone has an idea for a new law.

   **B.** The President signs a bill into a law.

   **C.** Congress votes on a bill.

   **D.** A bill is introduced to Congress.

**2.** What is Congress?

   **A.** a bill that becomes a law

   **B.** a group of leaders who make laws

   **C.** a type of traffic law

   **D.** an idea that will become a bill

**3.** What are the two parts of Congress?

   **A.** The Senate and the White House

   **B.** The House of Congress and the Governors

   **C.** The Senate and the House of Representatives

   **D.** The House of Representatives and the Voters of America

**4.** What happens when a bill is vetoed?

   **A.** It becomes a law.

   **B.** It is signed by the President

   **C.** It is introduced to Congress.

   **D.** It is rejected.

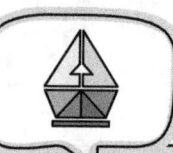
*Yesterday you learned how laws are made. You know that there is a special lawmaking process in the United States. Government leaders vote on bills. Those bills can become laws. Today you will learn about the 3 branches of government. They all have a part in the lawmaking process.*

**Directions:** Read the text below. Then answer the questions that follow.

Remember that bills are voted on by Congress. Congress members are part of the **legislative branch**. The **executive branch** makes bills into laws. The bill is sent to the President who is part of the executive branch. The President makes sure or **enforces** that citizens follow the laws. A group of judges from the **judicial branch** evaluates the laws. These judges make sure that the laws are fair.

# 3 Branches of Government

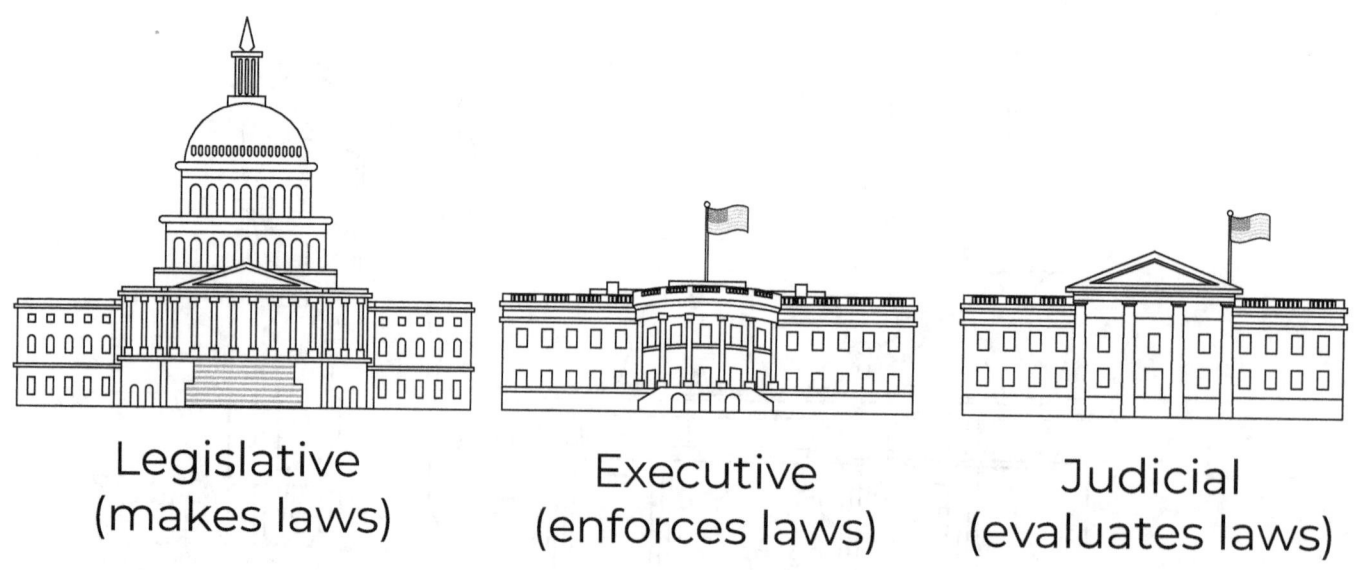

Legislative (makes laws)      Executive (enforces laws)      Judicial (evaluates laws)

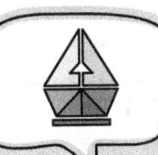
**1.** The ............................................. branch enforces laws and makes sure citizens follow them.

**2.** The ............................................. branch votes on bills to make them into laws.

**3.** The ............................................. branch evaluates laws and makes sure they are fair.

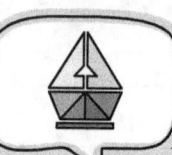
**Directions:** Read the text below. Then answer the questions that follow.

You know about the lawmaking process in America. Imagine that a friend wants to know how laws are made in this country. Explain the process in your own words below.

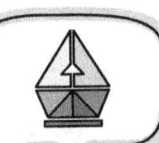
**Directions:** Read the text below. Then answer the questions that follow.

This week you learned about laws and how they are made. Today you will review what you have learned.

1. Which branch evaluates laws?

   **A.** judicial

   **B.** legislative

   **C.** executive

   **D.** all of these

2. Which branch is the President part of?

   **A.** legislative

   **B.** senate

   **C.** executive

   **D.** judicial

3. Who is part of the judicial branch?

   **A.** House of Representatives

   **B.** Congress members

   **C.** judges

   **D.** the President

4. True or false?

   The President has the power to reject laws.

   **A.** true

   **B.** false

# Civics & Government

## Citizenship

Learn about ways to be a good citizen in your community.

ARGOPREP

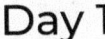
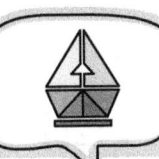
*Last week you learned about laws. You know citizens must follow laws as a part of good citizenship. Good citizens help make their communities a nice, safe place to live. This week you will learn ways to be a good citizen in your community.*

**Directions:** Read the text below. Then answer the questions that follow.

> Good citizens not only follow laws, but they also take care of their community. They make sure that the **environment** is safe. The environment is everything around you, including the air, water, plants and animals in your community. Good citizens make choices that will protect the environment. They keep the air and public property clean. They also do not harm community animals or plants.

**1.** What is good citizenship?

   **A.** living in the same place for a long time

   **B.** keeping your community safe and clean

   **C.** following the community laws that you like

   **D.** moving to a new community

**2.** Who is being a good citizen?

   **A.** a boy who is throwing rocks at trees

   **B.** a girl who is drawing on a park bench

   **C.** a driver who is ignoring the speed limit

   **D.** a family cleaning up trash at the beach

**3.** Which of these is NOT a part of the environment?

   **A.** a sweater

   **B.** a flower

   **C.** a duck

   **D.** a river

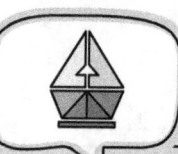
**Directions:** Read the text below. Then answer the questions that follow.

"

Remember that laws keep the community safe. Some laws and rules are made in order to protect the environment. Good citizens follow these laws.

"

Look at each sign below. Explain how each law protects the environment.

1.

........................................................................

........................................................................

2.

........................................................................

........................................................................

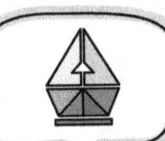

**3.**

..............................................................

..............................................................

**4.**

..............................................................

..............................................................

..............................................................

..............................................................

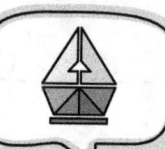
**Directions:** Read the text below. Then answer the questions that follow.

You know that good citizens follow community laws. They make sure that the environment is safe. Unfortunately, not everyone is a good citizen. Some people break laws and destroy public property. They do not care for community animals and plants.

Look at the table below. Read about each community citizen. Think about the type of citizenship that they show. Check the box for good or bad citizenship.

| | good | bad |
|---|---|---|
| Hector likes to take his dog Charlie to the park. He always makes sure that Charlie wears a leash. He wants to make sure that his pet and other people are safe. | | |
| Lisa loves to go jogging. She drinks water to stay cool. Sometimes, she does not feel like throwing her empty water bottles away. She tosses them onto the sidewalk. | | |

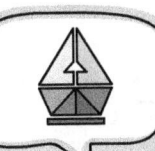
| | good | bad |
|---|---|---|
| Kisha is swimming at the community pool. She wants to practice her diving skills. Kisha sees a sign that says "No Diving." She decides to use the stairs to enter the pool instead of diving in. | | |
| Timothy wants to buy a baseball cap. It costs $20, but he only has $14. Timothy decides to take the hat from the store without paying for it. | | |

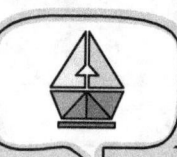
*Yesterday you learned about good vs. bad citizenship. Today you will think about yourself as a good citizen in your community.*

**Directions:** Read the text below. Then answer the questions that follow.

**1.** Describe ways that you show good citizenship in your community.

.......................................................................................

.......................................................................................

.......................................................................................

.......................................................................................

**2.** How do laws in your community keep you safe?

.......................................................................................

.......................................................................................

.......................................................................................

.......................................................................................

**3.** Imagine that you saw someone showing bad citizenship in your community. How could you help them be a good citizen?

.......................................................................................

.......................................................................................

.......................................................................................

.......................................................................................

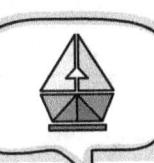
**Directions:** Read the text below. Then answer the questions that follow.

This week you learned about good citizenship. Today you will review what you have learned.

1. What is the environment?

   **A.** everything around you
   **B.** the people who live in your home
   **C.** the city that you were born in
   **D.** a place far away from your community

2. Which of these laws/rules keeps the community safe?

   **A.** stop signs
   **B.** park rules
   **C.** traffic laws
   **D.** all of these

3. True or false?

   Air is a part of the environment.

   **A.** true
   **B.** false

4. True or false?

   All citizens are good citizens.

   **A.** true
   **B.** false

# WEEK 14

# Civics & Government
## Rights & Responsibilities

Learn about the rights and responsibilities of community citizens.

ARGOPREP

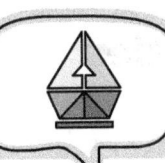
*Last week you learned about good citizenship. You know good citizens follow laws and take care of their community. This is part of a citizen's **responsibilities**, meaning things they must do.*

**Directions:** Read the text below. Then answer the questions that follow.

Being a citizen is not all about following rules or laws. All citizens have special **rights**. Rights are things that you can do. For example, American citizens have the right to free speech. They can say what they think and feel about important topics. This is called **freedom** of speech. Freedom is the right to do something freely without being punished.

1. What are rights?

    **A.** Things that citizens cannot do.

    **B.** Things that citizens can do.

    **C.** Things that citizens must always do.

    **D.** Things that citizens should never do.

2. What are responsibilities?

    **A.** Things that citizens do not want to do.

    **B.** Things that citizens should do sometimes.

    **C.** Things that citizens must do.

    **D.** Things that citizens can do once a week.

3. American citizens have *freedom* of ........................................... .

    **A.** speech

    **B.** driving

    **C.** jail

    **D.** all of these

4. Explain what freedom means.

...........................................................................................................

...........................................................................................................

...........................................................................................................

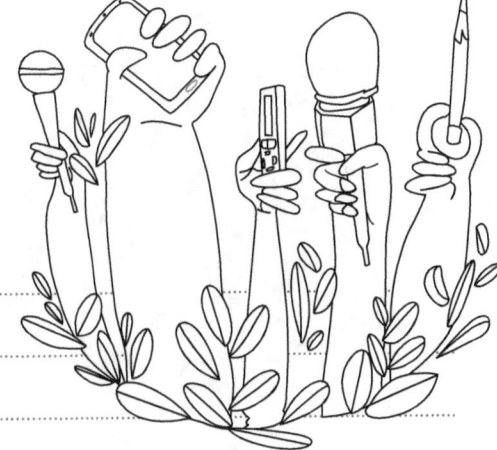

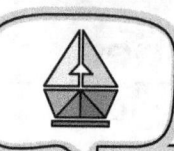
*Yesterday you learned about rights and responsibilities. Rights are things that citizens have the freedom to do. Responsibilities are things that citizens must do. Today you will explore the difference between rights and responsibilities.*

**Directions:** Read the text below. Then answer the questions that follow.

Look at the table below. Read the sentence on the left. Decide whether it is a right or a responsibility. Check the correct box.

| | Right | Responsibility |
|---|---|---|
| American citizens must follow all government laws. | | |
| All Oak Elementary students must wear uniforms daily. | | |
| Students may bring their own lunch or choose a meal from the cafeteria. | | |

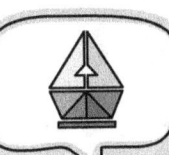
|  | Right | Responsibility |
|---|---|---|
| All homeowners in this town must pay property taxes. |  |  |
| Adults 18 and older are allowed to vote. |  |  |

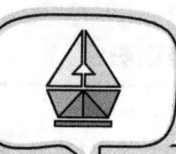
**Directions:** Read the text below. Then answer the questions that follow.

You know that citizens have rights and responsibilities. In America, there is a **Bill of Rights** that describes what people can do. The Bill of Rights was written by James Madison in the late 1700s. The **Constitution**, the supreme law in America, had already been written. But American leaders wanted to make rights and responsibilities more clear for citizens.

The Bill of Rights gave Americans new special rights, including freedom of speech, freedom of the press, and the right to a fair trial. People can say, write or publish their opinions. If someone is arrested for a crime, they have certain rights in court.

**1.** Who wrote the Bill of Rights?

   **A.** Abraham Lincoln

   **B.** Thomas Jefferson

   **C.** James Madison

   **D.** George Washington

**2.** What is the Constitution?

   **A.** the national flag of America

   **B.** the supreme law in America

   **C.** the supreme court in America

   **D.** the freedom of speech in America

**3.** Why was the Bill of Rights written?

   **A.** to replace the Constitution of the United States

   **B.** to take away citizens' rights and responsibilities

   **C.** to make citizens' rights and responsibilities more clear

   **D.** the purpose of the Bill of Rights is still unknown

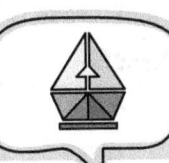
**4.** List 1 right that Americans have from the Bill of Rights. Explain what it means.

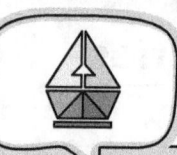
*Yesterday you learned about The Bill Of Rights. It shows what American citizens have the right to do. Today you will think about rights/responsibilities that you have as a citizen. This could be at home, at school, in your community, etc.*

**Directions:** Read the text below. Then answer the questions that follow.

**1.** I am a citizen at/of ........................................................................................

....................................................................................................................

....................................................................................................................

**2.** What rights do you have as a citizen?

....................................................................................................................

....................................................................................................................

....................................................................................................................

**3.** What are your responsibilities?

....................................................................................................................

....................................................................................................................

....................................................................................................................

**4.** Why are these rights and responsibilities important in your community?

....................................................................................................................

....................................................................................................................

....................................................................................................................

....................................................................................................................

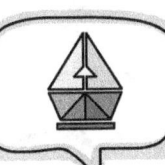
**Directions:** Read the text below. Then answer the questions that follow.

This week you learned about rights and responsibilities. Today you will review what you have learned.

1. Which of these is a responsibility?

   **A.** All citizens must obey city traffic laws.

   **B.** All citizens may give public speeches.

   **C.** All citizens may write newspaper articles.

   **D.** none of these

2. When was the Bill of Rights written?

   **A.** in the early 1400s

   **B.** in the late 1700s

   **C.** in the mid 1900s

   **D.** about 10 years ago

3. The Bill of Rights gave Americans freedom of ................................................. .

   **A.** speech

   **B.** press

   **C.** a fair trial

   **D.** all of these

4. True or false?

   Americans have freedom of speech, but they cannot write or publish these opinions.

   **A.** true

   **B.** false

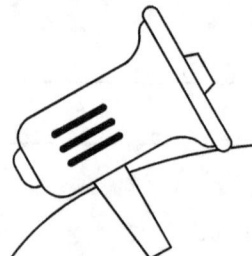

# WEEK 15

# Civics & Government

## Human Rights

Learn about the history of equality and civil rights in America.

ARGOPREP

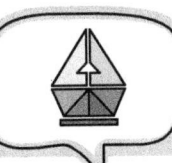
*Last week you learned about rights and responsibilities. You know American citizens have special rights. The Bill of Rights was written many years ago. During this time, all Americans did not have the same rights.*

**Directions:** Read the text below. Then answer the questions that follow.

The Bill of Rights introduced 10 **amendments** to the Constitution. An amendment is a small change. Remember that these changes gave American certain rights. However, some people did not have the same rights. For example, women and slaves could not vote. Over the years, more amendments were made. After slavery ended in 1863, the 15th amendment was written, giving African-American men the right to vote. Years later in 1920, the 19th amendment gave women the right to vote.

**1.** What are amendments?

    **A.** small changes

    **B.** male voters

    **C.** responsibilities

    **D.** old laws

**2.** Which amendment gave women the right to vote?

    **A.** 15th

    **B.** 12th

    **C.** 19th

    **D.** 10th

**3.** True or false?

The Bill of Rights gave all Americans the right to vote in the 1700s.

    **A.** true

    **B.** false

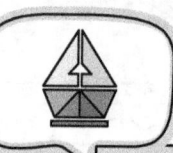
*You know some Americans did not have the same rights years ago. Women were not allowed to vote.* **Activists** *worked hard to make this change during the Women's Suffrage Movement.*

**Directions:** Read the text below. Then answer the questions that follow.

"

   The Women's Suffrage Movement began in the 1800s. It was led by activists such as Elizabeth Cady Stanton and Susan B. Anthony. They believed that men and women were equal. They wanted to have the same rights as American men. In 1848, activists held a large meeting called the Seneca Falls Convention where they talked about plans to help women gain equal rights. They had parades to gain the attention of lawmakers. The Women's Suffrage Movement went on for many years, and it later led to the 19th amendment.

"

**1.** What is an activist?

   **A.** someone who does not have rights

   **B.** someone who works hard to make changes

   **C.** someone who lived many years ago

   **D.** someone who wants things to stay the same

**2.** What was the main purpose of the Women's Suffrage Movement?

   **A.** Women wanted to write a new Constitution.

   **B.** Women wanted to have fancy parades.

   **C.** Women wanted to have equal rights.

   **D.** Women wanted men to stop voting.

**3.** What was the Seneca Falls Convention?

   **A.** a large meeting

   **B.** a small parade

   **C.** an activist

   **D.** a new amendment

*Yesterday you learned about the Women's Suffrage Movement. Activists worked hard so that women could have equal rights. Today you will learn about the Civil Rights Movement.*

**Directions:** Read the text below. Then answer the questions that follow.

"

Remember that slavery ended in 1863. Many years ago, African slaves were brought to America in the 1600s where they were forced to work for colonists. Slavery continued for many years. After it ended, former slaves were granted freedom. They could now have jobs and buy property. But many people still did not think African-Americans should have equal rights. These people did not want blacks and whites to live or work together.

In the late 1800s, people made laws to keep blacks and whites separate. This was called **segregation**. Jim Crow laws divided people by color. They could not live in the same community. They could not eat at restaurants together or drink from the same water fountains. Civil rights activists wanted to end segregation. They marched and gave speeches. They went to segregated restaurants and would not leave. Their efforts soon led to the end of segregation laws in the 1960s.

"

**1.** What were segregation laws?

**2.** How did the Civil Rights Movement help to end segregation?

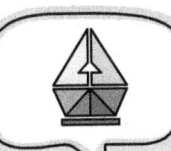
*Yesterday you learned about The Civil Rights Movement. You know activists wanted all people to have equal rights. People were divided by color due to segregation laws. Today you will learn about Martin Luther King, Jr., a leader in the Civil Rights Movement. King led marches and gave speeches. His most famous speech was "I Have a Dream."*

**Directions:** Read the text below. Then answer the questions that follow.

Read part of King's speech below.

"And so even though we face the difficulties of today and tomorrow, I still have a dream. It is a dream deeply rooted in the American dream.

I have a dream that one day this nation will rise up and live out the true meaning of its creed: "We hold these truths to be self-evident, that all men are created equal."

I have a dream that one day on the red hills of Georgia, the sons of former slaves and the sons of former slave owners will be able to sit down together at the table of brotherhood.

I have a dream that one day even the state of Mississippi, a state sweltering with the heat of injustice, sweltering with the heat of oppression, will be transformed into an oasis of freedom and justice.

I have a dream that my four little children will one day live in a nation where they will not be judged by the color of their skin but by the content of their character.

I have a dream today!"

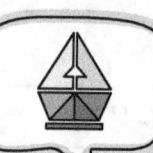
**1.** Explain why you think this speech was important.

**Directions:** Read the text below. Then answer the questions that follow.

This week you have learned about human rights. You know it is important for all people to have the same rights. Today you will review what you have learned.

1. When was the 15th amendment written?

    **A.** after slavery

    **B.** before slavery

    **C.** during slavery

    **D.** none of these

2. Who was a leader of the Women's Suffrage Movement?

    **A.** James Madison

    **B.** Martin Luther King, Jr.

    **C.** Susan B. Anthony

    **D.** all of these

3. What was Jim Crow?

    **A.** laws that ended segregation

    **B.** laws that divided people by color

    **C.** laws that gave women the right to vote

    **D.** laws that were written in the Bill of Rights

4. What was Martin Luther King's famous speech?

    **A.** I Have a Dream

    **B.** Dreams in America

    **C.** Martin's Dream

    **D.** I Dream of Freedom

# WEEK 16

# Economics

## Basic Needs & Wants

Ice Cream

MENU

Learn about the important things that people need to survive on Earth.

ARGOPREP

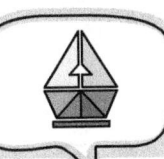
*You have learned many things about the way people live. You know about culture, community and citizenship. Today you will learn about **basic needs**. These are the things that people need in order to live.*

**Directions:** Read the text below. Then answer the questions that follow.

> Humans need 4 main things: water/food, air, clothing and shelter. We cannot live without them. Our bodies need water and food for energy. Our lungs need air to breathe. Clothing protects our bodies from the weather. Shelter, such as a home, also protects us from elements like rain and freezing weather.

1. What are basic needs?

   A. the things that people would like to have
   B. the things that people do not need
   C. the things that people need to live
   D. the things that people buy as gifts

2. Which of these is a basic need?

   A. shelter
   B. jewelry
   C. video games
   D. skateboards

3. Why is clothing a basic need?

   A. It is important to be stylish.
   B. It keeps people safe from the weather.
   C. It is nice to buy clothing as a gift.
   D. It is not important to wear clothing.

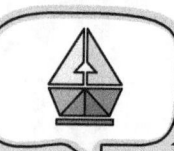
*Yesterday you learned about basic needs. These are things that people need to live. Today you will learn about **wants**. These are things that are nice to have but are not necessary for our survival.*

**Directions:** Read the text below. Then answer the questions that follow.

> Remember that people need food/water, air, clothing and shelter to live. Other things, such as toys and electronics, are wants. They make our lives more fun. People buy them for **entertainment**. Some wants can even make life easier. For example, people buy cars to travel. Driving is much faster than walking. But people can live without cars. They are just a **luxury**, not a basic need.

**1.** Which of these are wants?

   **A.** water

   **B.** television

   **C.** shirt

   **D.** apartment

**2.** True or false?

   People need cars in order to travel.

   **A.** true

   **B.** false

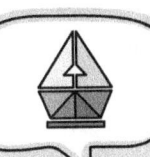
**3.** Explain why people buy things they do not need.

........................................................................................................

........................................................................................................

........................................................................................................

........................................................................................................

........................................................................................................

........................................................................................................

........................................................................................................

........................................................................................................

........................................................................................................

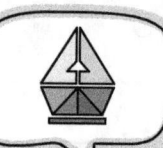
**Directions:** Read the text below. Then answer the questions that follow.

Remember that people have needs and wants. Sometimes, it may be hard to tell the difference. When you really want something, it can feel like a need.

Imagine you are walking past an ice cream shop. You see a delicious sundae through the window. You might feel a strong need to eat that sundae! Your mouth starts to water, and you begin to feel hungry. Your body is telling you that you need to buy it. But the truth is that ice cream is not a basic need. It is something you enjoy, but you can live without it.

Look at the table below. Think carefully if the item on the left is a need or a want. Write *need* or *want* on the right.

| Item | Need or Want? |
|---|---|
| swimming pool | |
| vegetables | |
| coat | |

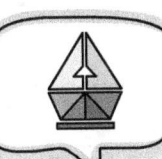
| Item | Need or Want? |
|------|---------------|
| chocolate cake | |
| cell phone | |
| house | |

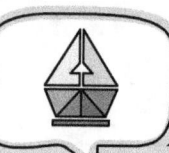
**Directions:** Read the text below. Then answer the questions that follow.

You know that people have needs and wants. Today you will think about your own needs and wants. Look around your home. What do you need? What is something you don't need but is very important or special to you. Write them in the chart below.

| My Needs | My Wants |
| --- | --- |
|  |  |

**Directions:** Read the text below. Then answer the questions that follow.

This week you learned about needs and wants. Today you will answer a few more questions about what you've learned.

1. Which of these is a basic need?

   **A.** candy

   **B.** diamonds

   **C.** music downloads

   **D.** none of these

2. What is a luxury?

   **A.** something that is fun to have but is not a need

   **B.** something that people cannot live without

   **C.** something that people need but is not very fun

   **D.** all of these

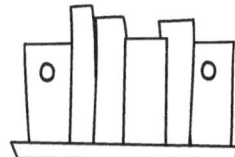

3. What is entertainment?

   **A.** things that make people hungry

   **B.** things that people buy or do for fun

   **C.** things that help people stay warm

   **D.** things that people need to live

4. True or false?

   Sometimes, people confuse needs with wants.

   **A.** true

   **B.** false

# WEEK 17

## Economics
### Natural Resources

Discover how people get the things they need from nature.

ARGOPREP

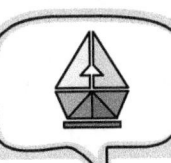
*Last week you learned about basic needs. People have basic needs such as air, water and shelter. People can use things from nature to meet their needs. These things are called **natural resources.***

**Directions:** Read the text below. Then answer the questions that follow.

> Natural resources come from nature. People use them to live. For example, rivers and lakes are natural resources. People use them as a water source to drink, bathe, etc. Plants and animals are natural resources that people use for food.
>
> Trees are also natural resources. People use wood from trees to build homes and make fires to stay warm. Plus, trees give us oxygen. Oxygen is a special gas that people need to breathe.

1. Where do natural resources come from?

   A. stores

   B. factories

   C. nature

   D. machines

2. Which of these is a natural resource?

   A. building

   B. ocean

   C. truck

   D. sink

3. How do trees help people live?

   A. people use them to build shelters

   B. people use them to make fires

   C. people get oxygen from trees

   D. all of these

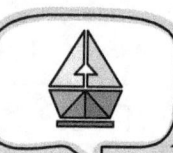
*Yesterday you learned about natural resources. People can use things from nature to meet their needs. You know that water and trees are natural resources. Today you will learn about more ways people use natural resources to live.*

**Directions:** Read the text below. Then answer the questions that follow.

People use natural resources for **energy**. Energy makes things move or work. The sun gives us light and heat energy. This energy can also come from **electricity**. Electric energy makes things (such as a television or a lamp) work.

People also use oil, gas and coal for energy. Oil, gas, and coal are all different types of **fuels**. Fuels are burned to create power and heat. Cars need the fuel of gas in order to move. Some stoves use gas energy to cook food. Factories burn coal to create electricity.

**1.** Energy makes things move or _____.

   **A.** stop

   **B.** work

   **C.** slow down

   **D.** freeze

**2.** Which of these can make heat energy?

   **A.** the sun

   **B.** electricity

   **C.** gas

   **D.** all of these

**3.** Which of these is a type of fuel?

   **A.** gasoline

   **B.** rain

   **C.** flashlight

   **D.** wind

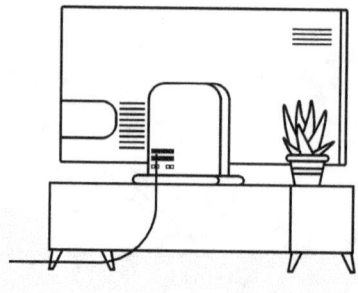

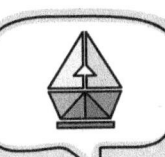
*You know people use natural resources for energy. Today you will think about how this energy is used in everyday life.*

**Directions:** Read the text below. Then answer the questions that follow.

Look at each picture and explain how natural resources are being used for energy.

**1.**

......................................................................................................................................

......................................................................................................................................

......................................................................................................................................

......................................................................................................................................

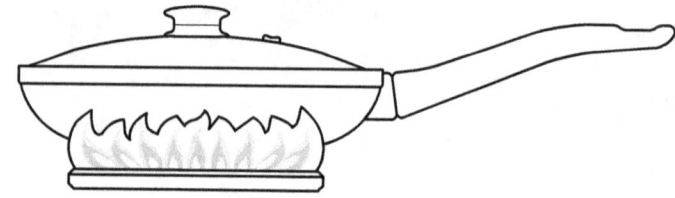

2.

...........................................................................................................................

...........................................................................................................................

...........................................................................................................................

3.

...........................................................................................................................

...........................................................................................................................

...........................................................................................................................

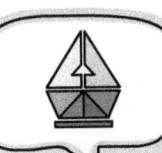
**Directions:** Read the text below. Then answer the questions that follow.

Today you will think about how you use natural resources. Write your answers in the chart below.

| | |
|---|---|
| water | |
| electricity | |

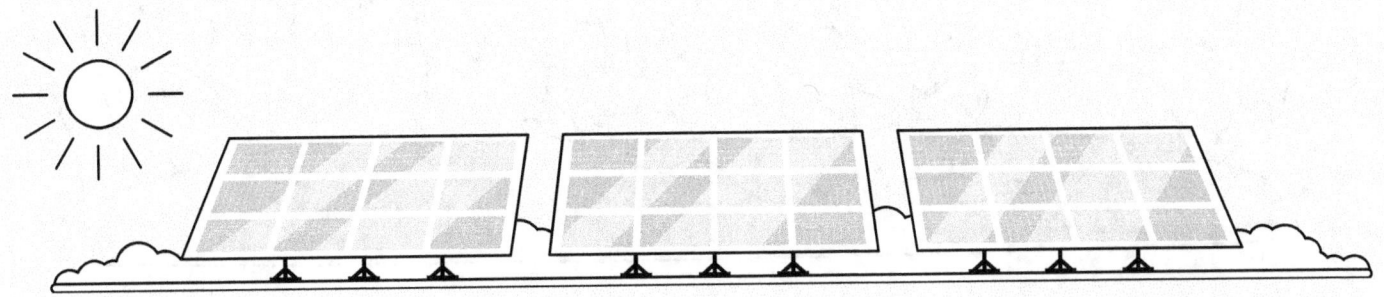

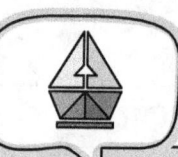
| | |
|---|---|
| plants | |
| trees | |

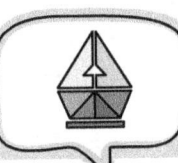
*This week you learned about natural resources. You know people need them to meet their basic needs. That is why it is important to **conserve** natural resources. This means we have to make sure we don't use too much water, energy, etc. so we can prevent running out of them.*

**Directions:** Read the text below. Then answer the questions that follow.

Visit The National Institute of Environmental Health website at https://kids.niehs.nih.gov. Here you will learn about ways to protect and conserve natural resources. Write a few sentences about what you learned below.

# WEEK 18

# Economics
## Goods & Services

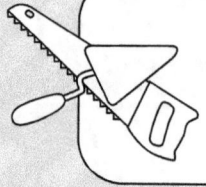

Learn about the things people buy to meet their needs and wants.

ARGOPREP

*You have learned about basic needs. You know there are certain things that people need to live. They can use natural resources, such as water and sunlight, to meet these needs. People can also buy their needs and wants.*

**Directions:** Read the text below. Then answer the questions that follow.

Have you ever gone to the grocery store? You may have seen food and lots of other **goods**. Goods are things that people can buy to meet their needs. Items such as clothing, food and tools are goods.

People also buy **services**. A service is something that someone does for you. For example, barbers give people haircuts. Doctors care for people when they are sick. These are services that help people meet their needs and wants.

1. _____ are things that people can buy to meet their needs.

    **A.** Services

    **B.** Energy

    **C.** Goods

    **D.** Wants

2. Which of these is a service?

    **A.** eating cheeseburgers at home

    **B.** getting your teeth cleaned at the dentist

    **C.** watching a movie at your friend's house

    **D.** driving home in your car

3. True or false?

    People pay for goods, not services.

    **A.** true

    **B.** false

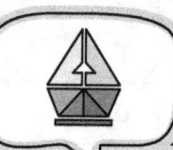
*Yesterday you learned about goods and services. You know goods are things that people buy. A service is something that is done for someone. Today you will explore the difference between goods and services.*

**Directions:** Read the text below. Then answer the questions that follow.

Read each scenario. Think about what each person is buying. Write **goods** or **services** on the line.

**1.** Tammy went to the shopping mall. She bought a jacket and a pair of shoes for $67.

.......................................................................................

**2.** Peter took his dog Fluffy to a pet groomer. The groomer bathed Fluffy and trimmed his fur for $45.

.......................................................................................

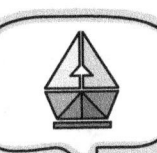
**3.** Mr. Washington went to the car wash. He paid the attendant $12 to wash and wax his car.

........................................................................................................................

**4.** Jen bought a bicycle helmet for $18 and a pair of knee pads for $9.

........................................................................................................................

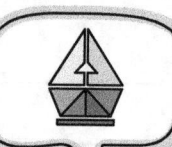
**Directions:** Read the text below. Then answer the questions that follow.

Remember that people can buy services to meet their needs. People who offer these services are usually paid. This service is their **job**. A job is work that someone is paid for. Sometimes people offer services for free. This is called **volunteering**. They offer services as a way to help others, not for money.

Jobs are an important way for people to make money. People use this money to meet their basic needs. They can buy the goods and services they need to live. Jobs also help the community. When someone is sick, they can visit the community doctor. Firefighters and police officers keep the community safe. That is their job.

1. A _____ is work that people are paid for.

   **A.** volunteer

   **B.** good

   **C.** job

   **D.** resource

2. People volunteer in order to _____ others.

   **A.** pay

   **B.** need

   **C.** meet

   **D.** help

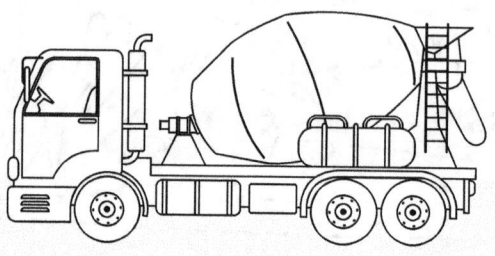

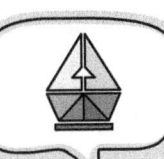
**3.** Explain how jobs can help the community.

........................................................................................................

........................................................................................................

........................................................................................................

........................................................................................................

........................................................................................................

........................................................................................................

........................................................................................................

........................................................................................................

........................................................................................................

........................................................................................................

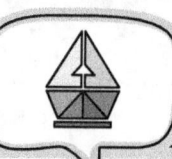
**Directions:** What is your dream job? Describe your dream job in detail below.

## My Dream Job

**Directions:** Read the text below. Then answer the questions that follow.

This week you learned about goods and services. Today you will answer a few more questions about what you have learned.

1. Which of these are goods?

   **A.** clouds

   **B.** apples

   **C.** lakes

   **D.** cities

2. Who is a volunteer?

   **A.** someone who works at a restaurant

   **B.** someone who is paid to mow lawns

   **C.** someone who sells lemonade for $1.00

   **D.** someone who rakes their neighbor's leaves for free

3. Which of these is NOT a job?

   **A.** teacher

   **B.** brother

   **C.** doctor

   **D.** firefighter

4. Who offers a service?

   **A.** someone who fixes cars

   **B.** someone who enjoys basketball

   **C.** someone who likes to read books

   **D.** someone who rides their bike to school

# Economics
## Producers & Consumers

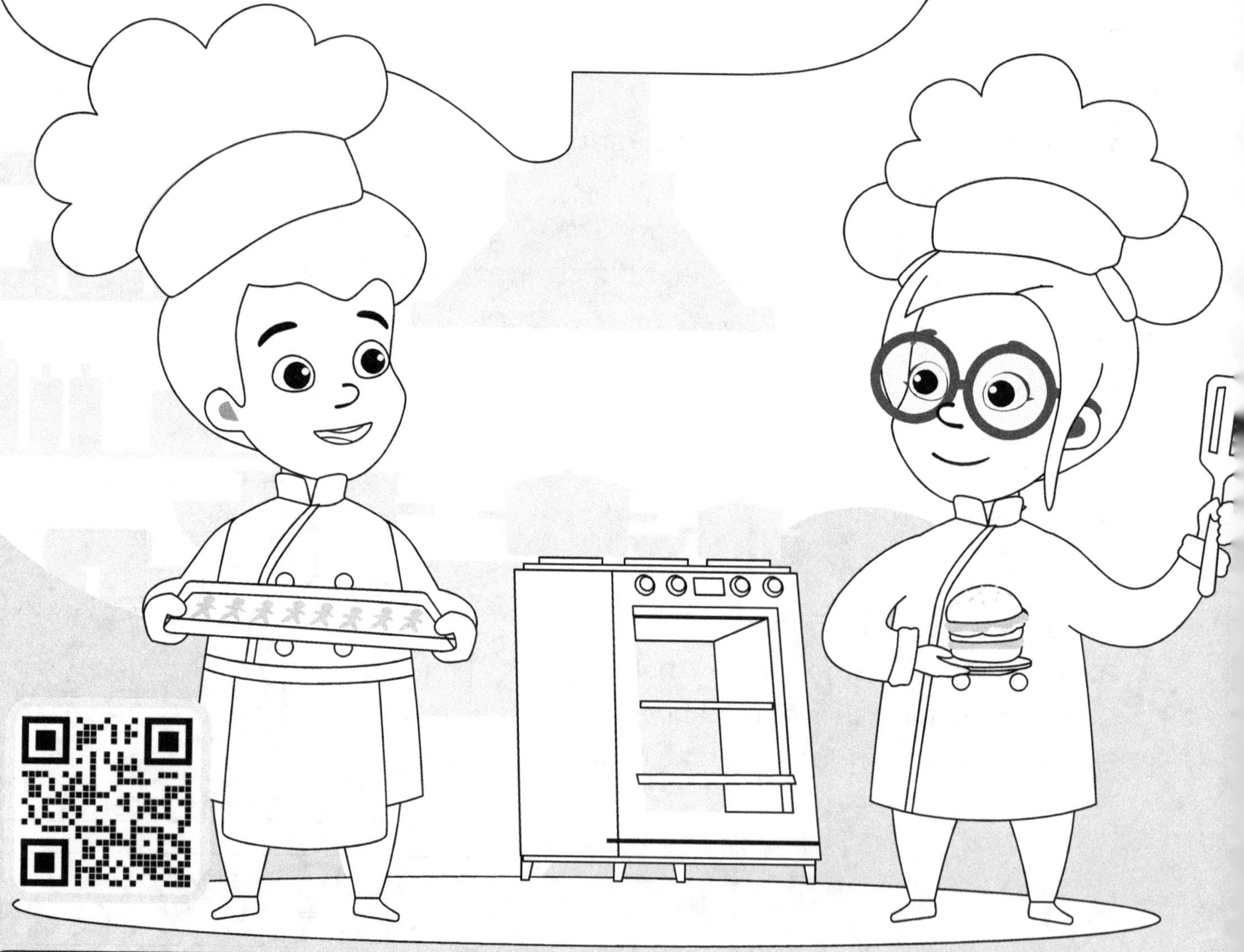

Learn about how people make, sell and buy things to meet their needs.

ARGOPREP

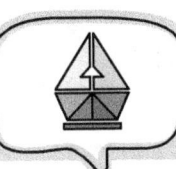
*Last week you learned about goods and services. People buy things to meet their needs. Jobs help people make money. They can use the money to buy the goods and services they need. People also use their jobs to offer goods and services. This week you will learn how goods and services are bought and sold.*

**Directions:** Read the text below. Then answer the questions that follow.

> The people who buy goods are called **consumers**. The people who make goods are called **producers**. Producers make goods and consumers buy them. This cycle continues in order for people to meet their needs.

1. Producers are people who ........................................ goods.

   **A.** buy

   **B.** eat

   **C.** make

   **D.** need

2. Which of these people is a consumer?

   **A.** Mark works at a factory that makes toys.

   **B.** Kim bought a bracelet from the jewelry store.

   **C.** Tia creates paintings and sells them.

   **D.** Olivia likes to bake brownies.

3. Why are consumers and producers both important?

   ........................................................................................................

   ........................................................................................................

   ........................................................................................................

   ........................................................................................................

   ........................................................................................................

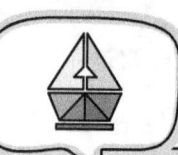
*Yesterday you learned about producers and consumers. You know producers make goods. Consumers buy goods. Today you will learn about this cycle.*

**Directions:** Read the text below. Then answer the questions that follow.

> Mr. Garcia is a farmer. He grows fruits and vegetables. He raises farm animals like cows and pigs. Mr. Garcia sells these goods to community grocery stores. People buy fruit, vegetables and meat from the store. Mr. Garcia produces more and sells it to the grocery store. More customers buy these goods.

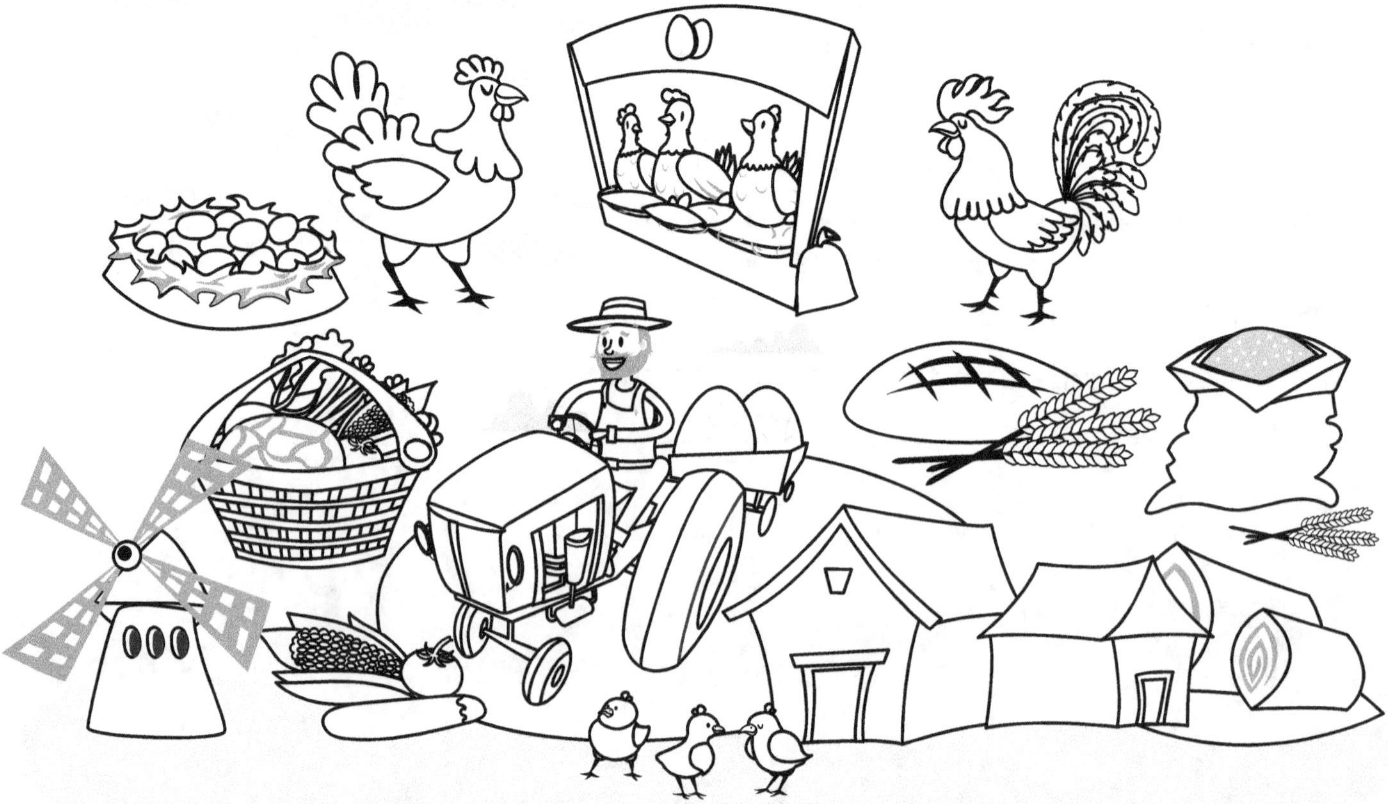

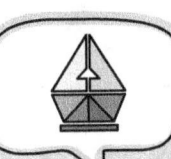
Show the cycle in this diagram. List each step in the appropriate box.

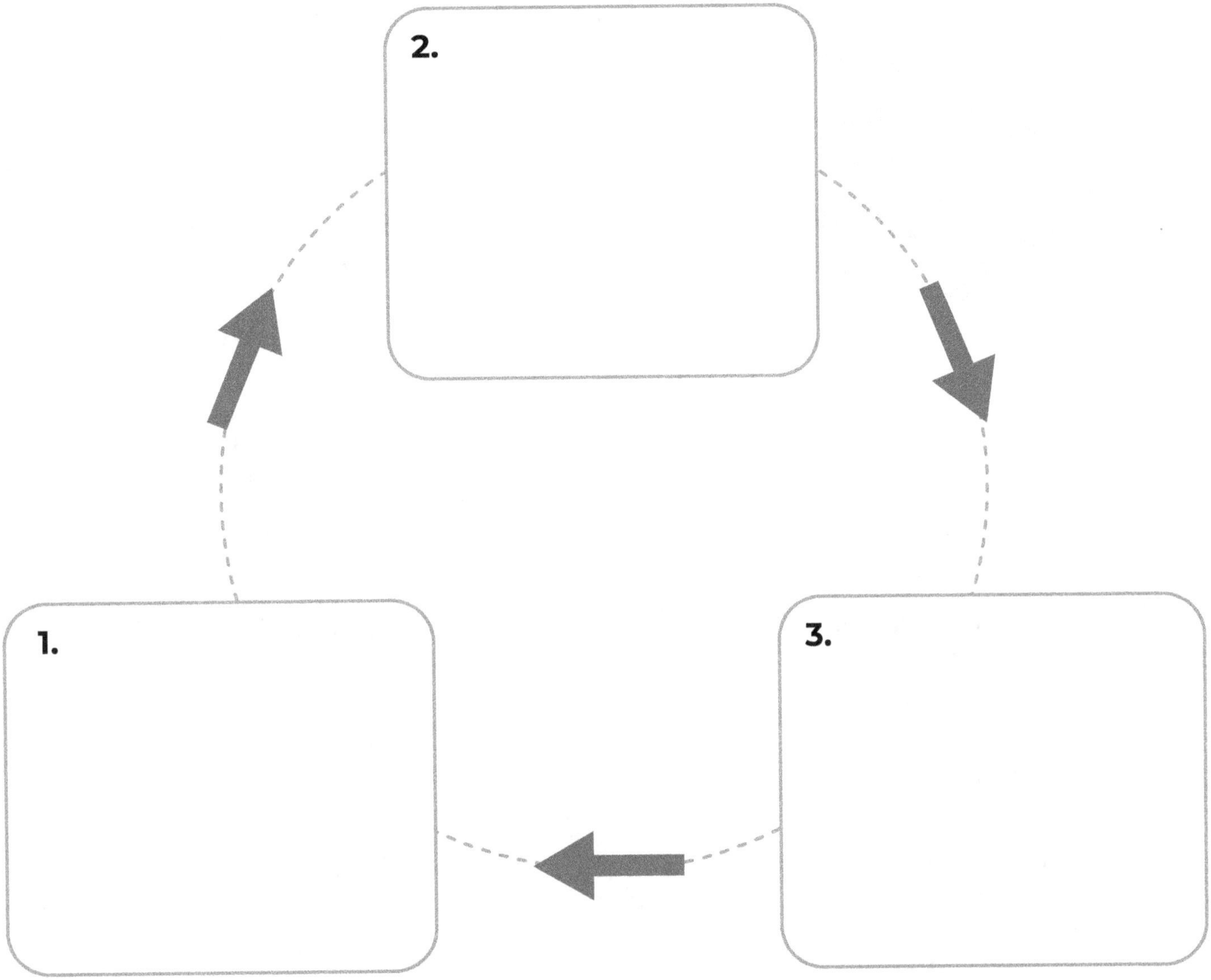

**2.**

**1.**

**3.**

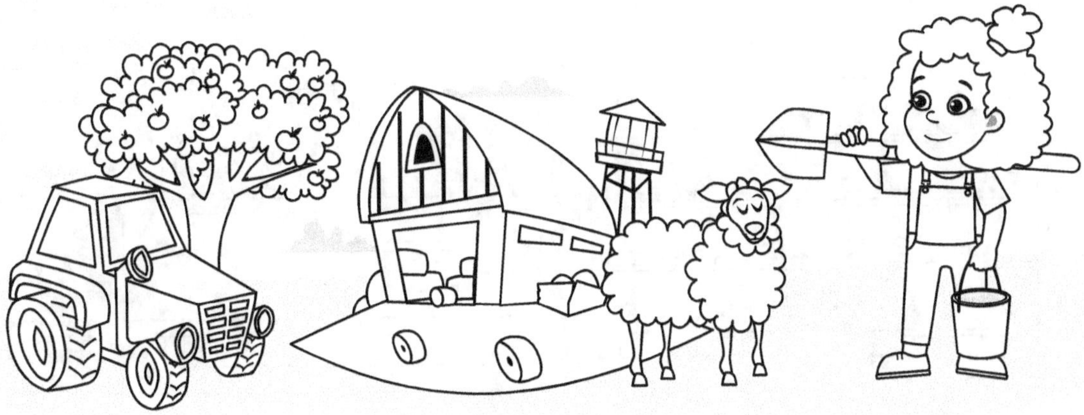

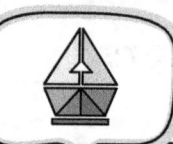
*Remember that producers are people who make goods. Producers can also offer services. Consumers buy these goods or services to meet their needs.*

**Directions:** Read the text below. Then answer the questions that follow.

"

Producers are **human resources**. They are people who use their skills to create goods or services. Producers need special things to do their jobs. These **capital resources** are goods that are used to make more goods. For example, construction workers build and fix things. They need hammers, nails, wood and other tools. These items are capital resources.

"

Look at each human resource on the left. Write a few capital resources they might need on the right.

| Human Resources | Capital Resources |
|---|---|
| chef | |

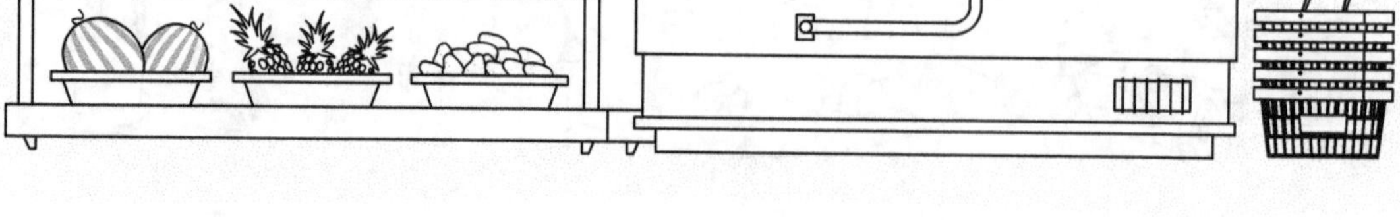

| Human Resources | Capital Resources |
|---|---|
| doctor | |
| hairdresser | |

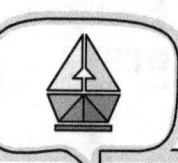
**Directions:** Read the text below. Then answer the questions that follow.

Last week you wrote about your dream job. Today you will think about what you would need to do that job. Make a list of capital resources below.

| My Dream Job | Things I Will Need |
| --- | --- |
|  |  |

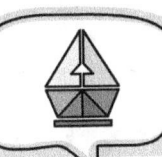
**Directions:** Read the text below. Then answer the questions that follow.

This week you learned about producers and consumers. Today you will review what you have learned.

1. What is the first step in the producer/consumer cycle?

   A. producers make goods

   B. consumers buy goods

   C. stores sell goods

   D. producers send goods to stores

2. What are human resources?

   A. people who use money to buy goods/services

   B. people who use their skills to create goods/services

   C. people who do not use goods/services

   D. none of these

3. Which of these is a capital resource?

   A. firefighter

   B. drill

   C. waitress

   D. baker

4. True or false?

   A janitor is a human resource. Mops, buckets and cleaning products are capital resources that a janitor needs.

   A. true

   B. false

# WEEK 20

## Economics
### World Resources

Discover how people around the world meet their needs.

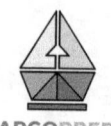

ARGOPREP

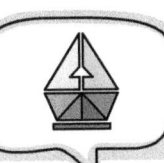
*You have learned about many types of resources. You know people need them to meet their basic needs. People have different needs around the world. This week you will learn how world communities meet their needs.*

**Directions:** Read the text below. Then answer the questions that follow.

> You know that people make and buy goods. Sometimes goods are made and sold in the same community. For example, a farmer might sell goods in a local store. Sometimes goods are produced in one community and sent to another. Producers **export** these goods to a place that is far away, like another country. Consumers in that country **import** the goods and use them or sell them.

1. What does export mean?

    **A.** to buy goods in a local community

    **B.** to send goods to a community far away

    **C.** to sell goods in your neighborhood store

    **D.** to use goods that come from other communities

2. Why do consumers import goods from other countries?

    **A.** to send them back

    **B.** to throw them away

    **C.** to use or sell them

    **D.** all of these

3. True or false?

    People only buy and sell goods in their own community.

    **A.** true

    **B.** false

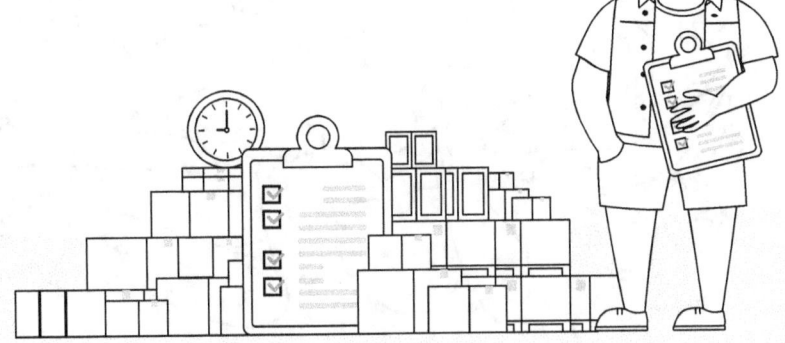

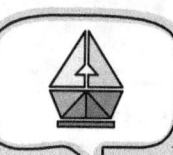
*Yesterday you learned about exports and imports. People buy and sell goods from communities all over the world. Today you will learn about why people buy and sell in different world communities.*

**Directions:** Read the text below. Then answer the questions that follow.

> People import and export goods for many reasons. Some resources are easier to find in a specific community. For example, certain fruits grow better in warm climates. It may be hard to find these fruits in a place where it is always cold. People need to import them from another country. Another reason why communities import and export goods is due to cost. Some countries may sell the same goods for a lower price. Often, this is because they have an excess amount of goods, meaning a **surplus**.

**1.** Why might someone import food from another country?

........................................................................................................

........................................................................................................

........................................................................................................

........................................................................................................

........................................................................................................

........................................................................................................

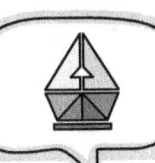
**2.** Why might someone export goods at a low price?

.............................................................................................................

.............................................................................................................

.............................................................................................................

.............................................................................................................

.............................................................................................................

.............................................................................................................

.............................................................................................................

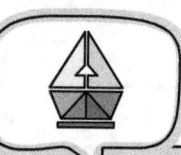
*You know people buy and sell goods all over the world. Some goods may be easier or cheaper to buy in certain places. Today you will learn about world communities and the goods they export.*

**Directions:** Read the text below. Then answer the questions that follow.

| Country | Main Exports |
|---|---|
| Japan | cars and electronics |
| Colombia | coffee, fruit and nuts |
| Africa | oil, gold, diamonds |
| United States | machines, oil/fuel |
| India | rice and gems |

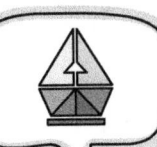
**1.** What are the main exports in Africa?

    **A.** cars and electronics

    **B.** rice and fruit

    **C.** oil, gold and diamonds

    **D.** nuts, rice and oil

**2.** Which country mainly exports cars?

    **A.** Japan

    **B.** United States

    **C.** Colombia

    **D.** India

**3.** Which country mainly exports coffee?

    **A.** United States

    **B.** Colombia

    **C.** India

    **D.** Japan

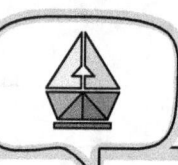
*Yesterday you learned about exports and world communities. Today you will think about the communities you live in. This could be your city, state, country, etc.*

**Directions:** Read the text below. Then answer the questions that follow.

Find out what the main exports are in your community.

**1.** Where do you live? What are the main exports of your community?

.......................................................................................................................................

.......................................................................................................................................

.......................................................................................................................................

.......................................................................................................................................

.......................................................................................................................................

.......................................................................................................................................

**2.** Why do you think people buy these goods from your community?

.......................................................................................................................................

.......................................................................................................................................

.......................................................................................................................................

.......................................................................................................................................

.......................................................................................................................................

.......................................................................................................................................

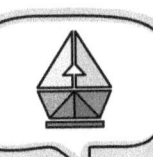
**Directions:** Read the text below. Then answer the questions that follow.

This week you learned about world resources. Today you will review what you have learned.

1. What are imports?

   **A.** goods that are received from other communities
   **B.** goods that are sent to other communities
   **C.** goods that are sent to local communities
   **D.** goods that are bought in local communities

2. What is a surplus?

   **A.** when a community runs out of goods
   **B.** when a community buys goods from other countries
   **C.** when a community sells too many goods
   **D.** when a community has an excess amount of goods

3. Why might people buy goods from other countries?

   **A.** the price is lower in another country
   **B.** the goods are hard to find in their own country
   **C.** the goods are easier to make or grow in another country
   **D.** all of these

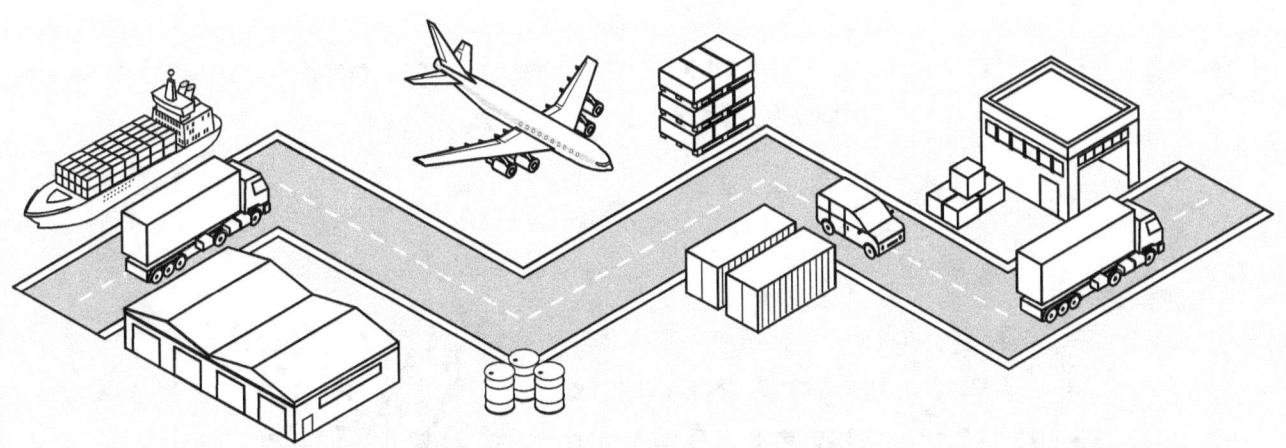

# Answer Sheets

To see the answer key to the entire workbook, you can easily download the answer key from our website!

*Due to the high request from parents and teachers, we have removed the answer key from the workbook so you do not need to rip out the answer key while students work on the workbook.

 To watch free video explanations go to: **argoprep.com/social3** OR scan the QR Code:

**Place your mouse over the workbook you have, and you will see the "Download Answers" button.**

For detailed video instructions on how to access the "Answer Sheets," please scan this QR code.

# Books explanations

All Books

Grade: **All**    Series: **Social Studies**    Search...

7th Grade Social Studies: Daily
Practice Workbook

5th Grade Social Studies: Daily
Practice Workbook

8th Grade Social Studies: Daily
Practice Workbook

4th Grade Social Studies: Daily
Practice Workbook

3rd Grade Social Studies: Daily
Practice Workbook

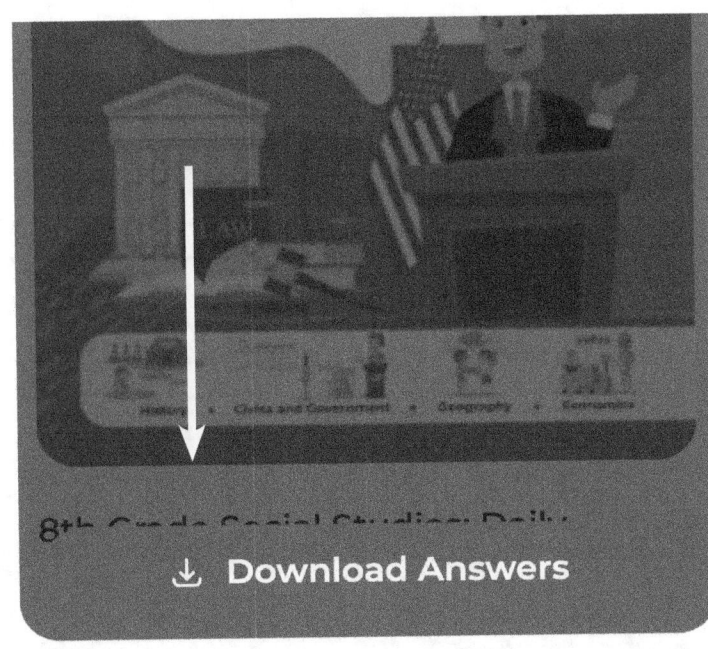

8th Grade Social Studies: Daily

⤓ Download Answers

4th Grade Social Studies:
Practice Workbook

www.ingramcontent.com/pod-product-compliance
Lightning Source LLC
Chambersburg PA
CBHW081329120626
46546CB00011B/3272